About the Author

Michaela Cummings grew up in Manchester, England, where she spent much of her teenage years. She moved from Manchester in the 1990s, when she began traveling in Europe, finally relocating to Toronto, Canada, in 2000. She became a Canadian citizen in 2008 and currently resides in Chatham, Ontario, with her husband, Ippolito.

Dedication

This book is dedicated to the people I lost between 2020 and 2023. They are greatly missed every day and will never be forgotten. Forever in my heart.

My dear mother, Norma Cummings; my uncle, Peter Cummings; my aunt, Carol Cummings; and my beloved friend, Georgianna Joseph. My beautiful brother-in-law, Massimo De Rose. My aunt, Shirley Batley, and my good friend, Colin Clark, who both recently left us in 2023.

I also dedicate this book to all the women who are struggling with their own menopausal journey. Hang in there, as you are not alone. Seek support and educate yourself. You've got this! To all the women who continue to discuss perimenopause, menopause, and post-menopause, keep talking! Women's health matters, and it is important to keep the conversation alive!

Michaela Cummings

THE MENO CHANGE DIARY

AUSTIN MACAULEY PUBLISHERS™
LONDON · CAMBRIDGE · NEW YORK · SHARJAH

Copyright © Michaela Cummings 2024

All rights reserved. No part of this publication may be reproduced, distributed, or transmitted in any form or by any means, including photocopying, recording, or other electronic or mechanical methods, without the prior written permission of the publisher, except in the case of brief quotations embodied in critical reviews and certain other non-commercial uses permitted by copyright law. For permission requests, write to the publisher.

Any person who commits any unauthorized act in relation to this publication may be liable to criminal prosecution and civil claims for damages.

All of the events in this memoir are true to the best of the author's memory. The views expressed in this memoir are solely those of the author.

Ordering Information
Quantity sales: Special discounts are available on quantity purchases by corporations, associations, and others. For details, contact the publisher at the address below.

Publisher's Cataloging-in-Publication data
Cummings, Michaela
The Meno Change Diary

ISBN 9798891551138 (Paperback)
ISBN 9798891551145 (ePub e-book)

Library of Congress Control Number: 2023924465

www.austinmacauley.com/us

First Published 2024
Austin Macauley Publishers LLC
40 Wall Street, 33rd Floor, Suite 3302
New York, NY 10005
USA

mail-usa@austinmacauley.com
+1 (646) 5125767

Acknowledgements

I would like to begin by thanking my husband, Ippolito, for his support, love, and understanding during the challenging moments I encountered when I transitioned into menopause.

I would also like to acknowledge my family and friends and express my thanks for their support, encouragement, and love during those difficult times of loss and grief.

Additionally, I would like to express my gratitude to Austin Macauley Publishers and their entire team for their invaluable assistance in making this book a reality. Thank you!

Table of Contents

Forgotten Fifty	11
Calabria, Italy	14
Toronto, Canada	20
50 Today!	33
Happy New Year 2020!	47
It's My Birthday!	106
Merry Christmas!	126
Back in Canada	152
Celebration Time: Come On, Let's Celebrate!	156
Aunty Carol's Funeral	161
European Final Come On, England!	169
Labor Day—Long Weekend	172
Merry Christmas!	181
New Year, New World: Happy 2022!	183
Italy!	188
Panic Attack	189
Vacation Day!	192
Happy New Year 2023!	198

Forgotten Fifty

Midlife came faster than I thought. Then suddenly, I was entering a whole new world and one which I was not prepared for. There was no education, resources, or guidance. It was me, myself, perimenopause, menopause, post-menopause. It was me with symptoms, mad hormones, health issues, and mood swings, to name a few. Suddenly I felt forgotten. I am no longer considered young or youthful anymore.

Midlife has come along and there is a big change, physically, mentally, and emotionally. I am not feeling this meno change and am having a hard time. I suffer in silence. Some days are better than others. Some days I wonder: *Is this it? Who do I turn to?* It seems women are more open about the subject nowadays. Still, for me, it is like a fork on the highway, and I am not sure which way to go.

Now, at fifty-three, it still seems like I am losing the battle of the pause. With continued bloating, night sweats, hot flashes, mood swings and sleep deprivation. It seems like it's never ending? I even still fight with food and sometimes wonder why I deprive myself of food. There is still a constant guilt when I indulge.

As I enter this midlife stage, I am not confident I can handle aging. I don't mean the physical side, looks or image. It is more in relation to how my body feels. There is such stigma put on aging, such pressure to remain youthful, even as the years pass. As a woman, you reach a certain age and you're finished according to societal standards. *Forty, that's where life begins,* I once thought. Does it though? At fifty, a woman is pretty much written off, especially if her hair is white or gray and no longer being dyed. A woman must look youthful to stand out.

Rather than listening to any of that nonsense, I know it is a blessing to have reached this age. There is so much hype around turning fifty. It is just another birthday if you are lucky enough to celebrate it. Now, when I look at the bigger picture, I have reached the ripe old age of fifty and I can only associate age with health, health, and health.

Being fifty and female, well, that is another story. A story where one reaches that perimenopausal stage in life. Followed by the menopause, oh and then post-menopause. There are far too many pauses, in my opinion, and lots to go through at this stage of life. Without any prior knowledge, education or help at hand, it hits like a flood and bam, a whole new life to adapt to. Some of us are over and done with it by their forties, others well into their fifties and beyond. If only I'd had more understanding around it all, I may have been able to embrace it a little more.

Instead, it feels like such a burden and a heavy one at that. I know many women struggle with the symptoms, yet each of us suffers in our own way. Talking with my female counterparts, we have so much in common. I am still trying to embrace this time and navigate through it all. For now, though, I take it one day at a time.

Although in 2018 I noticed changes, things really started to change for me in 2019, when I was forty-nine. My feelings, my mood, my body, and my menstrual cycle. I was just waiting for the time to pass, then I would officially be in menopause. Little did I know about all the symptoms and turmoil that would lead up to the menopause and beyond.

Calabria, Italy

June 2019

It all started in Italy in 2019, when my husband and I had decided to spend some time there with his family. Naturally, being one of my favorite destinations for the last thirty years, I was not going to refuse. I was always in a happy place when I was in Italy.

This time around, it was different; it's where the changes started happening, including the onset of perimenopause. Here I was, enjoying the sun, sand, and the beauty of Calabria, yet I felt low, very low. I could not understand why I was feeling so down. The sun was shining, the waves of the calm ocean glistened with the reflection of the sun. I felt a deep sense of hopelessness, like my world had ended. I was in Italy, I should have been feeling great and happy living my Bella vita. For a period, I was, and then it stopped.

When I look at my life, I should not have anything to whine or complain about. I have a husband that is easygoing, kind, genuine and would give me the moon if I wanted it. Yet here I was in Italy feeling a bit of resentment toward him. Unsure why I felt this way, it felt like I had no control over my mind.

My thoughts were fuzzy at times and my brain seemed to be in pieces. Why was I experiencing this overwhelming feeling of emotion? Is this a sign of aging? Am I on the change? I've heard about the change, but is this the start of something bigger? Is this something to be excited about? The mere thought of it all makes me tired. I understand that this is only the beginning.

I first noticed on June 10, 2019, a change in my monthly cycle. I was spotting here and there; it was not a full cycle. The previous month, there was nothing, I did not have my monthly. After a conversation with my girlfriend, she said she had missed six months and then had a period. *This must be the start of a change for me*, I thought, *a transition to my new reality*. The predictability of my cycle was over, and I could no longer know the exact date or when it would occur.

This was not good as we had booked a cruise at the end of June, and I was hoping I would be period-free for my travels. Or at least by mid-June. On June 30, I would be getting ready to embark on an eleven-day Greek island cruise, and there would be nothing worse than having the time of the month interrupt my vacation. It got to the middle of June and still I did not see any sign of my monthly.

It was not until June 24, five days before I was leaving for my cruise, that my period appeared, talk about the wrong timing. At this point, I only hoped it would be a light period. I did not know what this cycle would look like. To my delight, it was not heavy, and it passed quickly. On the day of my cruise, I was feeling alright, and it wasn't so bad. It can be such a burden when you go on vacation, and you have this on your mind.

Finally, the day arrived, and we were off to Rome for one pre-night in a hotel. We would travel by bus from Cosenza to Rome, which took around five hours or so. We would make numerous stops en-route. The good thing for me was, I was not as worried on this day as my period was light and I was reaching the end of my cycle, at least I hoped I was. We arrived in Rome later that afternoon with luggage in tow, welcomed by hot and sticky thirty-degree weather. We checked into our hotel and, later that evening, went out to eat dinner. Oh, to be in Rome!

I felt good at this moment and was looking forward to the next day. We had an early night because the following morning we would take the early train to Civitavecchia. When we arrived early the next morning, we found our way to the port in time for our pre-departure point on our cruise. So far so good, there were no heavy menstrual concerns.

So, we were off on an 11-day cruise, things looked positive. I would be able to swim, eat, and enjoy the cruise without worrying about my cycle. What a relief it was knowing I could enjoy myself.

We boarded and made our way to our cabins. I was OK. In fact, it was smooth sailing all the way around, and I was able to enjoy the splendors of Santorini, Mykonos, Athens, Crete, Portofino, and the rest of the cruise without total paranoia. It felt wonderful to be free and not have to run to the washroom every minute. I was living my best life, experiencing one of my greatest enjoyments, cruising.

This was my third cruise, and I hoped many more were to come, including a world cruise someday. Italy and Greece are two of my favorite places in Europe, and I knew the islands and the food would not disappoint. This was our first cruise on the Norwegian Jade cruise line. I have to say the service was spectacular and the crew just had so much energy. They knew how to please passengers. My mood was great, and I was enjoying my time. The eleven days sped by.

Our last day was as amazing as the rest, and we looked forward to eating dinner for the last evening in the company of some friends we made on the cruise. There would be a group of six of us dining together for the last night of the cruise. We would leave the cruise the following morning, before spending another post night in Rome.

After returning to our cabin on the last day, it seemed my menstrual cycle had different plans for me that night. For me, it did not look pretty. I spent the entire night in my cabin and could not make it for dinner. I had a seven-day period all in one night. I began bleeding, and it would not stop. I spent much of that evening in the bathroom. What on earth was happening here and what kind of timing was this? I could never have imagined it. I was bound to my bathroom. Is there even such a thing as a one-day period?

So, that was my last night on what had been a fabulous cruise. My husband went out for dinner and brought me back some food. This all happened on the tenth of July, and we would disembark on the eleventh of July. I managed to survive that night, and we headed to our hotel in Rome for one night.

Once again, I had hoped I could enjoy a day in Rome. That was not to be. Instead, I was worried about my period continuing and not being able to move around as freely as I would have liked to. I spent much of my time needing to use the restroom. When we reached St. Peter's Square, I just had to sit down and let my husband look and take pictures. I was exhausted, not only from the heat, but I just did not feel good.

As much as I wanted to enjoy the delights of Rome for my post-cruise night, on this occasion, it was not meant to be. In my eyes, my time was wasted, and at this point, I didn't know what was next to come. I knew my body was changing, but it seemed not for the better. Is this what I could expect on the change? My body seemed like it was just all over the place.

The journey back to Calabria the next day was a difficult one. The heat was blistering as we made our way to the bus terminal. My physical condition was poor, and I was concerned about the five-hour journey on the bus. At least there was a bathroom onboard, and we made a few bathrooms stops along the way. I did not feel so great.

At forty-nine, was this the start of a midlife crisis? Only time would tell. Midlife comes faster than you think. Then wow, it is here. Now what? I am almost a half century old, and that seems ancient to me. Oh my god, I am entering the club. Am I really going to be fifty years old? Yes, it is real. How was I twenty-one yesterday and today I am forty-nine? I cannot believe the passage of time. I'm seeing and feeling changes in my body. Who said growing old was fun?

The aches and pains, the days when you feel great, outnumbered by the days when you don't. An unpredictable menstrual cycle wreaking havoc on your cycle. After the episode on the boat, I would now be in constant paranoia about if my monthly was coming or not. For much of my life, my cycle has been regular as clockwork. Those days were now gone, and this was my new reality.

July 26, 2019
Today, I felt excruciating cramps and I started to wonder what was going on. I first started having these kinds of cramps when I was thirteen years old. As I was nearing

fifty, I never thought I would still experience such aches at this age. It takes me back to when I was at school, and I had to be excused because of the pain. It was unbearable, the only thing that helped was putting a hot water bottle on my stomach.

At that time, I suffered almost every month. When I awoke, I would always feel so much better than when I climbed into my bed. At my current age, I did not expect to experience this pain all over again. My only thought was, what is really happening with my body now? As I neared fifty, things continued to get progressively worse. Each month, I seemed to notice more unwelcome developments. These changes were only the beginning for me and more would come.

Toronto, Canada

In August 2019, I arrived back in Canada, only to experience further perimenopausal symptoms.

My world has changed over the last eight months. I have not been sleeping well at all. Could it be because I drink too many caffeinated beverages throughout the day? Probably. I have never been someone who gets eight hours of sleep a night. Well, not since being in my youth when those days I could sleep for twelve hours and even more.

Nowadays, I am lucky if I get two or three solid hours of sleep. My sleep pattern is all over the place. When I go to bed at ten, by eleven thirty-five, I am awake out of the blue. Once up, my overactive mind makes it a real struggle to fall back asleep.

Eventually, I do nod off, only to find myself waking up again at three or so to go to the washroom. On my best nights, I can attain up to 5 hours of sleep, and that is rarely solid. At times, I wish I could sleep like my husband. He is gone to the world in less than ten minutes.

Meanwhile, it is a struggle and a constant battle for me. One minute I feel the hot flash, and, in another minute, it subsides. Still, I toss and turn, feeling hot and bothered. The sweats come and go, just like the covers are on or off. When I wake in the morning, I feel more exhausted than before I went to bed. Now I do love a cup of coffee in the morning.

Maybe this will have to change. If I give it up, is that going to be my solution?

August 16, 2019

I couldn't sleep last night. When I initially opened my eyes, it was one thirty-eight. I tried to sleep again, but at four thirty, I needed to use the washroom. I went back to my room, but I couldn't sleep. I closed my eyes anyway, only to wake at 6 a.m., hot and sweaty. Another night with disrupted sleep.

This appears to be my current situation and I am feeling it each waking day. Wait, I feel another hot flash coming on as I write. My arms and head suddenly feel an overwhelmingly hot sensation. Who said aging was fun and growing old gracefully should be something embraced? I disagree with this now. Is this something that I will need to endure for the foreseeable future? There is no timeline, and that's the sad part. It all seems so grim. All this middle-age stuff.

August 18, 2019

Yet another night, I am awake at 2:38 a.m. and need to visit the washroom again. Even as I fight with myself, I cannot get back to sleep, it is simply not happening. I think I consumed too much caffeine during the day, but what can I expect?

The truth is, I like drinking something caffeinated in the morning to get me going and keep me awake. I probably don't need more than three cups, though. This might be the issue. Perhaps I will have to cut down on the coffee and see if it can ease my sleep troubles. At four thirty I am again wide awake, and my head feels heavy. I will just stay in my bed and close my eyes. One hour later, I wake up with a migraine. Is this all related to the perimenopause? Or the disruption of my sleep the result of excessive caffeine consumption? It's all starting to take a toll on me.

August 19, 2019

Lack of sleep is my new normal. It's driving me nuts. This morning, when I woke up, I had a slight migraine. The hot sweats haven't stopped coming during my sleepless nights and I feel like screaming. It's challenging for me, and every morning I wake up exhausted. When I look in the mirror, I see that my eyes have extremely dark rings around them. My sleep troubles are all I can think about these days. I'd do anything to get a few uninterrupted hours of solid rest. I need to change some of my habits, I know that. It's just sometimes easier said than done. Perhaps I will try and drink less caffeine today. We will see how it goes.

August 20, 2019

Wide awake once again. It is 1:58 a.m. I had one decaf coffee yesterday and a peppermint tea to see if that would help with my sleep. If I am honest, I am not sure if it really helped. Today I will try and go caffeine-free to see if I can sleep better.

I really need something. This sleep pattern is destroying me. My head feels extremely heavy in the front; it aches. If I am honest, I am not sure how much more of this I can take. I'm now starting to feel ailments throughout my body. It must be related to this change my body is undergoing.

August 21, 2019

I decided to abstain from caffeine entirely today in the hopes that my sleep issues would improve. It appears that avoiding caffeine had little effect on how well I slept. At around 2 a.m., I was wide awake once more. I'm trying to close my eyes again, but it's not working. Perhaps I require more than one caffeine-free day. The previous four nights were dreadful. I may need to improve my bedtime routine. I tried listening to some soothing music, but it didn't help. I can't seem to make anything work. I'll have to keep trying.

During conversations with my husband, he tells me it's all in my head. That's an easy statement to make when you go to bed and fall asleep in ten minutes. My situation is unique; if he were going through what I am right now, he might think differently. I wish he could walk in my shoes and experience the harsh reality. I don't believe I'm exaggerating.

August 28, 2019

Another night of lost sleep, just like the previous night. I drank far too much caffeine during the day. I am just not ready to give up on coffee yet. I know until I make the change, I will not see any results with my sleep. For now, I will continue to work on it.

As we approach the end of the month, I am still waiting for my monthly menstrual; my last one was on July 24, it is now August 28. My cycle is still so unpredictable right now. I had gone six weeks without my period and then one came. I then had a one-day event and a gap of two weeks. I am all over the map in that area. I am still having menstrual migraines and stomach cramps as well. There's a lot going on down there right now. At times I just feel low, like there is no hope for my sleep and my feelings to improve. I am tired and struggling each day, depending on my mood.

August 30, 2019

Did I even sleep last night? I never feel like I have had a good night's sleep. In fact, I cannot remember the last time. My nights are pretty much the same now: restlessness, tossing, turning, and a sudden whoosh of heat taking over my body. Everything is consistent.

Today though, I feel fine, and my mood is OK. My emotions have been a little erratic at times, but I am trying to adjust to all this change. Sometimes my situation appears very bleak. Then there are moments when I feel better. I am all over the place. Nothing, not even the beautiful country of Italy, seemed to be able to lift me out of the darkness of my thoughts and feelings during this period in my life.

My moods change by the minute and when I am in the deep low feeling, I cannot seem to shake it off. I have no control. Then there goes another hot flash in the span of thirty seconds. This is my new world, and I don't like it. I think I am going to schedule a doctor's appointment. Let's see if she has any advice that can make me feel a bit more upbeat about the situation. I really hope so.

Meanwhile, the hot flashes are still ever present and might continue for years. If that's the case, what a daunting prospect. *Accept change and always see the bright side of things, Michaela.* If only it were that simple. (I'm getting hot as I write this.) With continued aches and pains, low moments and unpredictable emotions, constant fatigue and sleepless nights, this is my perimenopausal journey. Each day is new, and I never know how I will feel until I wake up.

September 1, 2019

It's a new month and today was a relatively good day with no hot flashes. It's too bad my last night's sleep was not good. Once more, I woke up in the middle of the night needing the bathroom and feeling hot. I just feel as if I am constantly in a light sleep, never fully sinking into unconsciousness.

At seven thirty-eight, I am awake again and sweating profusely. I need to get up and have a shower. I am not loving this endless saga of disrupted nights. But who wants to be hot and sweaty, irritable, and groggy from continued lack of sleep? I just want a few hours, is that too much to ask for?

September 4, 2019

Hallelujah, I believe I slept for a few hours last night. I was awake at 3 a.m. for a bathroom trip, then again at 4 a.m., and then I finally got some shuteye before waking up. Even though I only had a few solid hours of sleep, it was still a good night. During this unpredictable time, I will treasure these nights because there aren't many of them right now. I wouldn't say my sleep pattern has improved drastically, but it appears to me that I slept for a longer period last night and I will embrace that.

Finally, I was able to schedule an appointment with my doctor. I'm hoping she can give me some advice or reassurance that I'm not alone in this. However, we have never had any in-depth discussions about what to expect during perimenopause or menopause.

During a consultation about a polyp removal a few years ago, I mentioned that I was starting to have hot flashes, and my gynecologist said that it was perimenopause. Professionals, it appears, use the word and that's it. From that point forward, you must navigate this word and its meaning on your own. I have no idea, knowledge, or education about the subject. I haven't even done a lot of research. Neither my mother nor any of my relatives ever brought up the subject.

From what I recall, it had never been discussed. "Oh, I think she's on the change," or "I think she's gone a little funny," are phrases I heard constantly around the subject and that was it.

September 7, 2019

My most recent sleep pattern is that I wake up with hot flashes after only a few hours in bed. I then close my eyes and force myself back to sleep. Sleep does not usually come easy. At 5 o'clock, I awaken again, tossing, turning, and sweating profusely. The sheets need changing. I sound like a broken record, but it is just ongoing.

On occasion, my day starts with a headache. Maybe my headaches have something to do with the change in the weather here in Canada? My body is constantly changing, and I can feel it. There always seems to be something wrong. I have a doctor's appointment this week, so I'll tell her about everything to see if anything can be done to provide relief from some of these symptoms.

My thoughts are racing these days, and I can't seem to focus on anything. I feel anxious at times. I find it difficult to concentrate and often forget where I put things. If I'm feeling good today, I might be down the next day. I am trying to take it in stride, but it is not easy to just roll with it all.

September 9, 2019

I feel OK today, but it seems to be the nights that are killing me. I cannot get a good night's sleep. It is so frustrating, along with the hot flashes and sweats. I continue to toss and turn. I thought my sleep pattern was getting better, but I guess it is just not. It seems like the sleep and sweats are worse. I know I should stop feeling so pessimistic about the whole thing. But it's not easy to be optimistic about it all. Today I will go and see my doctor. I hope she can give me some helpful suggestions.

I am sitting in the doctor's office waiting to be seen. I am just sweating as I wait. A sudden rush is overtaking me in a flash. *Breathe*, I say to myself, *OK, here we go*. My turn. I speak to my doctor and give her the rundown of what I seem to be experiencing these days. She tells me that with being perimenopausal, there is not much she can do. There are some herbal remedies, but they are not guaranteed to work. She also mentions that there are some anti-depressant medications that may help, but they do have side effects. The side effects may ease what I am experiencing.

In my mind, I thought, *No way. I am not taking any medication for depression.* I am not a person who is quick to reach out for a pill to remedy my ailments; I would rather handle the situation on my own if that is all that is on offer.

I will, however, get blood work done to see if I am enduring the perimenopausal stage.

At fifty, my Dr. did mention other examinations which I would need to have. There is just so much to look forward to. Bone density, pelvic ultrasound, mammogram. I get it. With age comes more checkups. Back to the perimenopause, I think I'll just have to work around it and do what works for me and my body.

September 12, 2019

What an exhausting night of tossing and turning! Every hour and a half, I was awake. I felt like I usually do when I don't get enough sleep. Is it, however, the coffee?

At this point, I am not so convinced. I need to come up with some alternatives or remedies. This stage of my life has introduced me to an entirely new sleeping game, one that is becoming increasingly difficult to manage. There is no light at the end of the tunnel for me. I've heard friends say black cohosh works for them, but I've read mixed reviews, so it might not work for me. If I truly want to see a change, I must make the change. When it comes to taking medication of any kind, I am always hesitant and a bit of a procrastinator. I will continue to suffer unless I take that next step.

September 16, 2019

Last night, I slept for four hours straight. Then the hot sweats broke out and I was awake. Eventually, I closed my eyes again after tossing and turning for about an hour. I know I'm not the only one dealing with this, but it's still not a fun time. I feel like I am in an endless cycle of lack of sleep. I still haven't had a menstrual cycle in over six weeks. I'm not sure when it will happen again.

My system is a mess, and I never know what to expect. The key is to always be prepared and keep emergency supplies in your bag. I'm about to turn fifty soon, and I'm not sure how I feel about it. My friends are already joking about having to pay more for travel insurance as you get older. My mind is racing right now, and it appears to be nothing new. I never paid that much attention to my age before.

Suddenly, I am approaching the big 50. Being a woman often brings so much stigma when you reach a certain age. Part of that is you are written off, or you are not good enough anymore. Your appearance is no longer youthful. Maybe that is what society is saying but it is so not true. Though I am seeing and feeling drastic changes as I reach this age, I have never thought much of trying to turn back time. What's that saying, grow old gracefully.

September 17, 2019

Hot flashes and night sweats have continued, so I tried to sleep in lighter clothing last night. I had been heavily perspiring all night, leaving me saturated the next morning. I can't stand it any longer. It's driving me insane.

I had some blood work done yesterday. Six bottles of my blood were easily sucked from my veins. My doctor and I will talk about her findings. I also have a pelvic transvaginal exam today, so I must wait another hour before using the restroom. This is traumatizing for me, and I try to suppress it. My previous experience with this exam was a nightmare.

When I arrived, I discovered that the exam could not be performed because the technician had called in sick. They then transferred me to a different location. Naturally, I was itching to use the restroom by this point. I proceeded to the next clinic. There wasn't much of a wait, thankfully. Then it was over in forty minutes. I've always had a weak bladder. I shudder at the prospect of having to take this exam whenever I need to. All this women's stuff can be exhausting at times. It's gotten even worse now that perimenopause has entered the picture.

September 21, 2019

Last night was another night of restless leg activity in sweat-soaked sleepwear. The covers were on me one minute and off the next. It was probably worse than the last few nights. They were not that good either. I felt shattered today. Just shattered and with no energy. The nights are too much, I am not sure how much more I can handle. But it is nothing new in my world these days. I cannot remember when I last had a decent night's sleep. My hot flashes seem to be in full force and are more prevalent than ever.

Today I am going to meet my girlfriend. I am currently sitting on the bus with the air conditioner flowing. I chuckle to myself as I relish the cool breeze tickling my skin. I am loving the feeling of this ride. Soon, however, my good mood is interrupted as the hot flash takes over me. What is going on? It is all too much. I feel like crying. Take a deep breath, I say to myself as I continue my journey.

September 22, 2019

In a few days, I will turn fifty, and I'm not sure how I feel about it. I suppose I could say I feel conflicted. On the one hand, I think, wow, have I really been alive for fifty years? Contrarily, I still feel young. My body might not agree with the young bit right now, but that is how things are. The aches and pains might change in the future, but that is something to be expected as we become older.

Although they claim that fifty is the new forty, I feel old some days. Can I handle getting older? I probably could but just spare me the hot sweats and let me have a good night's sleep. As well as the sleep, my mind is still wondering about the next menstrual cycle. It has been almost two months since the last one.

To be honest, from my conversations with other women, anything can happen. I am perimenopausal now, but I have got to go the whole twelve months without a cycle, and then I will be in menopause. Oh, wait, then there is post-menopause. This can go on for years. Oh, what a thought. We each have our own stories and experiences with it all, which seem similar in so many ways.

I wish I could be more upbeat about everything. I'm extremely pessimistic and negative about it all. But I am just honest and that is how it is. It is not all roses and flowers right now.

September 24, 2019

Of course, last night was another agonizing one in which I awoke at 3:30 a.m. and then tossed and turned. I decided to get up at 7 a.m. My ever-changing body is a foreshadowing of what is to come. Recently, I've also noticed that my stomach is acting strangely. It's making a lot of gargling sounds. Maybe it's because I'm hungry? My body appears to be changing and going haywire daily. My breasts were extremely tender for a few months, then they felt like heavy bricks. They appear to be fine for the time being.

I'm gradually adjusting to this new phase of my life. Now I understand that diet and food consumption must play a larger role in my life. These days, I'm attempting to be more aware of my portions. My problem is that I enjoy those chips so much that I can't just eat a few; I must finish the entire bag. I feel compelled to eat more when the food is good, simply overeating for pleasure and failing to listen to my body.

I spent the first eight months of 2019 in Italy with my husband. In Italy, the food and festivities were plentiful. Pizza, pasta, bread, and other delectable foods which are simply too good to pass up on. Simply living the 'bella vita'.

Who, after all, can resist Italian cuisine? The only issue is that if you are not careful, you could gain a lot of weight.

Now that I'm back in North America, the food tastes different. I know I need to pay more attention to my diet. For starters, the sweet stuff must now be restricted. I'm still consuming caffeinated beverages, but I don't consume a lot of alcohol. I can take it or leave it when it comes to alcohol.

My desire has never been strong, and I have never felt compelled to drink to be happy. I'm also keeping an eye on my midsection. My diet has a big influence on this. I'm more conscious of what I eat now. I miss the days when I didn't have to think about such things.

50 Today!

September 25, 2019

My big birthday is today. The year I was born was 1969, a man walked on the moon, and I now wear reading glasses. I'm fifty years old and, to be honest, I'm not sure how I got here. Time flew by and then suddenly, I was fifty. But, at the same time, I am grateful to be here. I'm still breathing.

I'm just living in the moment and will keep my birthday simple and low-key. I'll have a nice dinner with some friends later. I had other plans, but plans do not always come to fruition in life. That is also acceptable. But who am I to complain when my husband gave me an eleven-day amazing Greek island cruise for my birthday in July?

This day is shared with my wonderful friend Georgianna. We were both born on this day and have both reached the age of fifty. Is it normal for me to feel old at fifty? When you say you're half a century old, you sound old. Time has flown by. It seems like only yesterday that I was carefree and fancy-free while traveling and living in Europe.

Today, however, the sun is shining, and I am feeling good. Surprisingly, I never know how I'll react to the perimenopause stuff these days. When I wake up and feel good, I know it's a good day, and I'll take it. I was born fifty years ago and am still trying to make sense of it all. But, hey, it's just a number, so what's the big deal? Just accept it. I'm dealing with it, as well as the other issues. I am also feeling thankful to see the day.

On Wednesday, September 25, 2019, the weather was sunny and warm in Toronto. What a beautiful day spent by the water and on a patio for lunch. Then it's on to another patio for dinner. A relaxed day to celebrate my fiftieth birthday with friends. It's been mostly free of hot flashes. It's now nearly midnight. I'm not sure if I'll be able to sleep well tonight.

With fifty, the symptoms continue: hot flashes, sleeplessness, sweats, moods swings, anxiety, ups and downs, highs, and lows. At times, it's still no fun.

The more I talk to people and read, the more I realize this seems to be the norm. We're all going through it in one way or another, with similar or dissimilar symptoms. We may be of different ages or have completed the cycle and are experiencing erratic changes.

But, at this point, we're all on the same train. I've been on this train for some months now, and what a train ride it is. I'm curious why there isn't more information out there about this stage in a woman's life and what to expect. You must simply deal with it when it comes around and you are pretty much on your own. I'm doing my best to deal with it all, one day at a time. I hope one day this situation will appear better.

October 1, 2019

I awoke this morning with a migraine. Another night of intermittent sleep. I'm drenched, and I can feel water dripping down my neck. Is this what it feels like to be fifty? I've accepted things; now I just need to get on with my life and not let this time get the best of me. Hot sweats, intense heat, the sensation that my face is turning color, and a lack of sleep are persistent. Every morning, I wake up to the same thing that happened the night before. Maybe I should try changing some of my habits and see how things go.

It's a new month, and the day began with a wave of hot flashes, which continued throughout. I wore my jacket, took it off, and put it back on, and that was pretty much how the day went. I just felt like I was constantly perspiring and overheating. I'm aware that my sleep patterns, cycle, and feeling hot are a constant battle, even though I am suffering in silence. I hope things will calm down. I still have not had a menstrual cycle.

I'm wondering if that's it for now. Is all this finally over with? I sincerely hope so. But I believe it is far too early to consider that. I have a follow-up appointment with my doctor on Thursday. Hopefully, everything is fine.

October 3, 2019

I had a follow-up with my doctor today, and everything seemed to be alright. My doctor did mention there were some things I should be more aware of. She said I need to pay more attention to my diet and lifestyle. Although I know that all too well, I still have days where I struggle with my diet, only to beat myself down when I fall off track.

My food choices need to be more consistent. My bad cholesterol has worsened, but it could be due to genetics. My fibroid is still 8 centimeters long. As a result, I'll need to return for a Sono hysterogram. The good news is that I only need to take two Advil tablets an hour before the procedure, as opposed to the pelvic ultrasound, where I had to drink water for up to an hour beforehand. Hopefully, they will see whether it has grown. I must say, I do not really feel any pain from the fibroid.

October 8, 2019

My nights continue to be horrendous, and my sleep pattern changes frequently. Last night I woke at 1 a.m., then 3 a.m. and then five. In the morning, I am exhausted, tired, and not feeling great. I am not sure how much longer I can take all of this as I am starting to feel drained. The only positive thing now for me is I am not employed. I am happy about this; I am not sure I would be able to cope with the routine. Especially when I am surviving with very little sleep.

My brain probably could not take commands. I finally got around to buying some herbal sleeping pills today. I think I will take one tonight and see if that aides me with my sleep troubles. I recall my doctor also mentioned in conversation that if I was having trouble sleeping, she could refer me to a sleep clinic. I think that would take too much effort.

October 10, 2019

Last night was another long night, even though I took a sleeping pill. It didn't seem to work because I woke up in the middle of the night again and needed to use the bathroom. I kept sweating profusely and the covers were on and off repeatedly. Perhaps I need to keep taking a sleeping aid for a while before I will see any results. But I think I'm just hoping for a miracle. Am I just overthinking all this sleep stuff? That is what my husband still thinks. I do not believe it's in my head. For me, it is very real. I am just surviving and trying my best day after day with little success.

October 13, 2019

I was surprised this morning when I looked at the clock and saw that it was 6:45 a.m. I couldn't believe what I was seeing. I went to bed around 1 o'clock, but for the first time in months, I seemed to have gotten a decent night's sleep. I'm talking about months. Maybe those herbal sleep aids were effective. A miracle occurred. I don't remember waking up two or three times during the night or tossing and turning. There were no hot sweats that I recall.

That was strange, because the last few months have been nothing but chaos when I tried to sleep. I wanted to scream and dance because I had finally gotten some longer, uninterrupted sleep. Is it true that I slept well last night? I simply couldn't believe it. I am still in shock. For this moment, I will rejoice about last night and hope for more wonderful nights of sleep like that.

October 14, 2019

Did I get too excited about my sleep last night? Yes, it was too good to be true to have two nights of better sleep. Once again, I woke up twice during the night. My hot flashes were back, and the covers were off and then back on again. I really thought I was onto something after the night before. I thought that my pattern was going to turn around from that point on and I would be able to have some good nights of sleep.

It's better to continue to take each night as it comes. It is all so unpredictable. I am having a bit of relief here and there from the daily hot flashes. This could be because I have been focusing on other things and not really thinking about it so much. A few weeks ago, it seemed like another story. I just feel helpless. Some nights I have four hours of sleep, give or take. When I get four hours, I can wake up and feel OK. I do not feel as wrecked as I usually feel. All I need, though, is consistency.

October 24, 2019

It's been three months since I last had a period. I'm hoping I'm on the right track to not having another menstrual cycle. It's been a while since I've had to buy sanitary products, which is a relief. I know I shouldn't get too excited, because anything can still happen at this point, and it could appear out of nowhere, according to many conversations with friends who are going through similar situations. One friend is 53 and still as regular as ever with her cycle. It's different for each of us women, as we experience different symptoms and go through different stages. It's hard being a woman sometimes.

October 25, 2019

Another sleepless night filled with hot flashes and profuse sweats. I awoke at midnight, 2 o'clock, and 4 o'clock. I attempted to go back to sleep and just lay in bed until sunrise. I couldn't sleep after 4 o'clock and was wide awake. Sleep was simply not happening for me, no matter how hard I tried.

My story isn't changing, and each morning seems to be the same; I'm not sure how much longer I can keep going like this. It's driving me insane, this never-ending saga. I use the term 'saga' because that is how my sleepless nights are currently. I simply believe there is no hope for me. I lack optimism and feelings of positivity when it comes to the subject of middle-age perimenopause. I've had enough of everything. All I want is to feel energized in the morning or well rested.

My sleeping pattern has changed yet again, and I am now waking up every three hours. In the third hour, I fall asleep and awaken. It wouldn't be so bad if this felt like a proper sleep that I could be proud of. It never feels like a restful night's sleep.

Unfortunately, I had no success with the herbal sleep aid that I tried a few weeks ago. I haven't tried another pill since. Maybe I should take them consecutively for a week or longer and see if there is any progress. Where is the help in all of this? There just seems to be no solid help or solutions. The library has books on menopause. I will just have to read up and see what different people are saying. Maybe I can find some tips or suggested remedies. Only time will tell.

November 1, 2019

It's a new month, and I'm completely exhausted. That's what a lack of sleep does to you. It causes fatigue and exhaustion. Sleep deprivation, night after night, will undoubtedly influence one's health, including mine. When I wake up in the morning and look in the mirror, I notice tired-looking eyes with dark circles, they seem to get worse with each passing day. I've just not been sleeping well for months, and it's finally starting to show.

I feel haggard and tired at times. I'd never noticed the dark, tired-looking circles under my eyes before. They now appear prominent when I look in the mirror at any given time. I don't think there will ever be an end to this. Can't I just return to my thirties or early forties?

When I turned fifty, I had no idea what to expect. My expectations for each month are not high. I can't even say I'm heading in the right direction because I'm not. At this point, I think I'll just have to keep researching all this meno stuff and try to come up with a plan that works for me.

November 3, 2019

Another night of agitation and bathroom trips. Sleep appears to be the most used word in my vocabulary right now. I had only one cup of tea during the day and decided to try another sleeping pill. It didn't work. It made me sleepy, but it couldn't provide me with five, six, or seven hours of sleep.

It's really starting to bother me. I need to try to do something. I only drank half a decaf coffee today. I will no longer consume more than one cup of caffeinated beverage per day, and I would like to see if this will help me. The next step will be to try to completely wean myself off caffeine.

To be honest, I'm not sure if this is the only problem. I am not good at making decisions and carrying them out on time. I think about it and procrastinate, but I never get around to doing anything about it. Even though my nights are disrupted, I am still taking my time to find the much-needed answer or resolution. It has already gotten to the point where I am suffering. I understand that to see any change, I must act.

November 12, 2019

My sleep continues to be erratic. While I try and sleep, my usual routine is waking up at 2, 4 and 7 a.m. Even though I feel as if I am in this light slumber, I am just lying in bed and not even sleeping. Even if I close my eyes and think I have slept, usually, I have not. Constant interruptions to go to the bathroom or feeling soaking wet with sweat pouring off me. Is this the most I can expect from my perimenopause?

It's terrifying, and my nerves are getting the best of me. I just want a good night's sleep. I'm not asking for much. Last week, I decided that I needed to wean myself off caffeine. My plan of action was to limit it to one cup in the morning and that was it. Words are not as powerful as actions. In the past, my doctor mentioned that I could go and do a sleep test at a sleep clinic.

This is where I'd be watched all night to see what was going on. The thing is, I'd never had trouble sleeping before, until I hit middle age. I was never the type of person who would put their head down and go to sleep; however, I did typically get six hours of sleep. Now, I'm lucky if I can close my eyes for two hours without waking up in the middle of the night. Then, once awake, I suffer the agony of being unable to return to sleep. In all honesty, I don't like the thought of being monitored in my sleep. I can be quite apprehensive at times.

November 15, 2019

It's morning again, and I'm still waking up in the middle of the night, tossing and turning. I was looking forward to my fourth month of menstrual freedom as November 24 approached. I guess I was thinking too big and getting ahead of myself.

On November 15, my stomach began to feel a little off, and when I went to the bathroom, I noticed a spot of blood. I noticed a brownish substance when I inserted a tampon. My stomach felt blah, again on November 16, and when I went to the restroom, some more blood appeared. I believe I am now dealing with this again, not knowing what to expect. Menopause, according to my doctor, is when you go a year without having a menstrual cycle.

As a result, the cycle has been broken. I'll just have to always keep pads and tampons on hand. I am hopeful that one day I'll be free of this menstrual upheaval and madness. Just when I thought I was on my way to menstrual freedom. I guess it's not over till it's over.

November 22, 2019

Today I went out and bought another stash of sanitary products again. I thought I was done with having to buy those things. I guess I am now back to square one. I finished my little period and now I am not sure what, where or when I will see my next one. I must keep in mind that there should be no spotting or period at all for a year. I guess I am not quite there yet. I never experienced any cramps; the period just came.

Now, I am not sure when the next cycle will be. I may not even have one again for some months. My cycle is all over the place, and it's changing constantly, and I seem to be feeling the physical changes. The hot flashes are back with a vengeance, and when I get four or five hours of sleep a night, I am excited. The problem is that those nights are still few and far between. My nights have maintained the same pattern of waking. I just cannot seem to get back to sleep. I tried the sleeping pill thing again and that did not seem to work.

Then I tried rubbing a natural remedy on my feet, which is supposed to help you relax and sleep. Sorry, it's not going to happen, and I'm not sure what else I can do. I know I must get the caffeine out of my system as soon as possible. I will just have to try harder. The fact is, I have had a few days with no caffeine, and I am still tossing and turning. I am still struggling as every morning I wake up feeling wrecked. Although this may be a time of change in a woman's life, it is quite something.

December 11, 2019

My sleep deprivation persists, although at times it seems slightly better. Still, I'm waking up at 3 a.m., which appears to be a popular time for waking up right now. I am finding these times ridiculous and difficult. I just muddle through each night and day with hope things will get better. My friend told me I should try some cannabis oil as this is supposed to help with sleep. I think I need some relief. I will have to investigate that. My issue is that I dislike taking medication if I do not have to. It may work for them, but will it work for me?

I'm still wondering if I'll have my monthly cycle. I'm not certain. My due date would be around Christmas, but it is not guaranteed that I will get it. My current thought is, "Will I or will I not?" To be honest, I'll just have to wait and see.

I feel my body is constantly changing, and I am losing bone mass. I need to start lifting some weights to strengthen and firm up. Sometimes it's hard to motivate myself. It always starts with my good intention, but it is usually not too long before my will runs out. It is consistency that will help.

I do have an appointment lined up for February to see my gynecologist. I had a polyp removed a few years ago, and it seems like I have another one. Not just that, I also have a fibroid which is about eight centimeters and has been around a while. It does not really cause me any discomfort, and the doctor says it should shrink as I go through menopause. I hope so, I am just waiting for this thing called the menopause.

December 28, 2019

It's already December 28 and the Christmas frenzy is over. As we approach the new year, I'm hoping that my infrequent menstrual cycle will return at some point. I suppose if I was still regular, I would have had a period on the 24th. My most recent period was in November. You never know what, where, or when you'll have another period in your fifties. I believe the key now is to always have some kind of sanitary product on hand, just in case.

My hot flashes are still persistent; daily they appear out of the blue. At times during the night, I am waking up with hot sweats again. In one minute, I am sweating so hard I need to take off a layer of clothing. It happens in the space of a moment. Some nights are more intense than others, but I am trying to cope.

My sleep is still not that great; I am always waking up at two or three-hour intervals. My struggle continues. I try not to think too deeply about it, but I really hope one day I can get back to having a good, solid sleep.

Currently, it seems like that is an illusion. No one prepared me for this roller-coaster change of midlife. I hate to always sound so bleak, but that's because it makes me feel this way. The thought drives me crazy. I just try and get on with it amidst the hot flashes. But they are still always there. Maybe next week will be better.

December 30, 2019

It's 4:43 a.m., and I can't sleep. My sleeping habits are still erratic. Even when I force myself back to sleep, I wake up around 3 a.m. most mornings. Then there are the nights when the restlessness persists. I've woken up soaking wet and sweating the last two nights. This could be contributing to the agitation. Then there's always the need to use the restroom. It's as if my body is set to wake up in the middle of the night.

This is my new normal, and even though it has been going on for months, I am still trying to adjust. I'm exhausted, drained, fatigued, and stressed out because of it all. I still haven't had my period, and it's the end of December. I'll just have to continue to make sure I have the necessary items on hand in case it appears.

My body changed so quickly once I hit fifty. My bones ache, my bat wings are just hanging in there, and I'm starting to notice cellulite. I never paid attention to all of this, now suddenly it seems to bother me. Breathe. It's OK. Isn't age just a number? It's not so much my age as it is how I feel.

Happy New Year 2020!

January 24, 2020
The month of January roared in like a lion and is continuing in the same manner. So far, this month has been full of surprises. My sleep was getting better, or so I thought. By better, I mean not waking up every two hours during the night.

At the very least, I'm getting more than three hours of solid sleep each night, which is exciting in my perimenopausal world. Hot flashes are still present and, at times, irritating. The restless legs and nights continue, and I wake up sweating profusely. I'm talking about full-on sweating and burning. Then clothing and sheets must be removed. I start feeling cold soon after, so I put the sheets back on. It's all in a night's sleep. It's been almost two months since I've had a period.

Two months have passed, but I doubt I'll be jumping for joy at this point. As I know, anything can happen. Let's just hope I can get through the third month without one, and then I'll be good to go. I'd like to add that these perimenopausal times are truly something. In my world, I had never known what to expect during this stage in my life. My body continues to fluctuate between hot and cold. Is this ever going to end, I think to myself. Even if it is not over, I only hope things improve, including my sleep, cycle, and night sweats.

So, January is over, and the month was no different from any other. I experienced the same symptoms. Tomorrow is another day and another month. Let me see if I can be a little more positive.

February 6, 2020

February has arrived, and I'm hoping not to see any signs of my menstrual cycle, but life is so unpredictable. Will I go another month without seeing anything in February? I can only hope so. It is February 6, and I'm starting to get a menstrual migraine. At times these migraines can be overbearing, and I need to take a tablet for relief when they occur. My focus over the last few months has been wondering whether I will see another period as I just don't know where I am at.

My health is at the forefront of my mind. I had a polyp removed about three years ago, and it appears that the polyp has returned. I have an appointment with my gynecologist on February 18 to see what is going on.

At this point, I'm not experiencing any discomfort, which is a good thing. I've never had any serious health problems. On occasions my iron levels have dropped, and I have taken some iron tablets to help me. Now, though, I am trying to manage my iron level with my diet. After a recent visit with my doctor, she was wondering why the ferritin level seemed low? I have an appointment with my Dr. again on February 20, so we can discuss that then.

February 7, 2020

Today I'm seeing brown spotting? I continued to spot on the eighth and ninth of February, and it was light. It's not a full-blown period, just some brown spots here and there. You need to go one whole year without any signs of bleeding or spotting to be in the menopause. That means I am not even close.

Although I consider myself fortunate to have reached this milestone fiftieth birthday, I am experiencing a slew of challenges that come with age. All this spotting and the irregularities in my cycle. Maybe I am at the tail end of it now. I am not having a heavy period anymore and that is great. It is just the uncertainty of not knowing what to expect. At this point, anything can happen.

On February 12, I had to take a fasting blood test. The results stated my ferritin levels had dropped even further. My doctor has asked me to follow up with her, that way we can look at what is happening. As I age, it seems like it's all about health and the body, doctor's appointments and issues related to my womanhood. Is this what aging really looks like? I remember being younger and joking about aging, now it's my new reality.

February 18, 2020

Today is my gynecologist's appointment. Our main topic of conversation during my visit was my period. My polyp is extremely small. The doctor suggested that we monitor it over time or remove it if it is bothering me. She welcomed me to the 50 club, and I figured it was all downhill from there.

I didn't have another period after my three days of brown spotting. She says my periods and perimenopausal symptoms all sound normal. So, she advised me to carefully monitor my menstrual cycle for the next four months and take note of any changes. I mentioned hot flashes and she said that was expected during this time. I was hoping for a bit more information but did not get it.

February 20, 2020

Back at my doctor's office on February 20, she was still perplexed by the sudden drop in my ferritin level and wanted to refer me to a gastroenterologist to investigate. All the other blood tests appeared to have been normal, except for the ferritin. I had already done the stool test; it came back normal, which was a relief.

Everything is a relief now when you get the results and they are positive, especially at this age. Health is at the forefront of everything, and life can be difficult without it. Your health really is now your wealth if you have it. My doctor has recommended I get a colonoscopy, which doesn't sound thrilling.

It does have to be done as part of the ongoing health checks, which seem as if they are never-ending at this stage. I know I have no choice in the matter, and I need to try and take charge of my health. I am really paying more attention than ever before. Bring back those carefree days when I could eat what the heck I wanted and not even care about my waistline, heart health and all the other stuff that comes with it.

For now, I'll just keep an eye on my menstrual cycle, and my doctor wants me to check my blood again in early March to see what's up. So, for now, I'm back to taking iron supplements. We'll see if this makes a difference.

I don't have to be concerned now. I just try not to worry and take each day as it comes. It's funny because, prior to reaching this milestone, I would frequently hear people in their fifties and older talking to doctors about how things were going downhill and such. I can relate to those things now that I'm there. I honestly have no idea what will happen with the menstrual cycle. We will just wait and see.

My girlfriend, who is the same age, has completely stopped, so no two women are the same during the perimenopause cycle. Some people get over it faster than others, while others just go through the motions. I'm still having difficulty sleeping because of the night sweats.

This seems to be ongoing; I wake up sweating and drenched each night. I am still hoping one day for a good night's sleep. Lately, I just continue to wake up feeling fatigued every day. Will this ever end? I wish I had been taught about this period of my life earlier.

March 7, 2020

My nights are always the same because I am exhausted and tired all the time. The dark circles under my eyes are a permanent fixture when I look in the mirror. However, this is to be expected with sleep deprivation. Tomorrow is a new day, and I'm hoping for a better one.

A Pandemic has been declared.

March 11, 2020

Right now, I, like the rest of the world, feel trapped in this bubble. Who could have predicted the current situation, this global pandemic? Certainly not me. Italy, the hardest hit country by COVID-19, has been terrible and heartbreaking to watch.

The southern part has not been affected as much as the northern part of Italy. My husband's entire family is in the south, currently under lockdown until April 18, which will almost certainly be extended. The funny thing is, we started hearing about COVID in the news as early as January 2020. Others and I were making light of it, not taking it seriously. To be honest, I doubt anyone did.

On March 11, 2020, social media videos of people fighting over toilet paper began to circulate. What on earth was going on? For god's sake, we were talking about toilet paper. It looked like toilet paper and hand sanitizer had become the best-selling items.

A new century has begun, and with it, a new pandemic. Toilet paper and hand sanitizer are driving people insane in North America and around the world. For the last three months, the story of COVID has been in the news, and nations have been slow to act and be proactive, resulting in a massive loss of life. What began in China quickly spread to Europe and the rest of the world. Italy has had the highest number of cases and deaths outside of China thus far.

Meanwhile, in Canada, all sporting events and large gatherings have been postponed, or canceled. Businesses are closing or changing their operating hours. Even with assurances that we have a reliable food supply chain, I noticed long lines and empty shelves while grocery shopping. Every day, more cases of COVID-19 are reported in Canada, though nowhere near the scale of our European counterparts. I've heard a lot about the economy and the stock market. But what about human life, which is far more valuable.

March 16, 2020

In life, you never know what's around the corner. Things are going along smoothly one minute, then something unexpected happens. In 2019, I spent months in Italy, taking advantage of the mild winter weather and exploring the country's most beautiful sights. I went on two wonderful cruises.

Now, I sit back and watch as many industries, including the cruise line industry, slowly deteriorate because of recent events. We were even planning our next Caribbean cruise for the end of this year. We'll have to put that on hold for the time being. However, a cruise can wait. Every day, people are dying because of this virus, which is extremely dangerous. I'm hoping we will be able to get through it, but these are now uncertain times.

On March 17, 2020, Ontario schools declared a state of emergency. Schools were closed, and restaurants could only offer takeout or delivery. We were all told to stay at home as much as possible, and the emphasis was now on social distancing. I noticed changes taking place in our way of life. Things were happening and changing so fast.

For now, I'm keeping an eye on things each day and turning on the news to keep up to date with what is happening. I am already dealing with my perimenopausal transition and for now, this is another added stress. As each day passes, I continue to follow the global response to this crisis.

Right now, death tolls vary from country to country and, in Canada, from province to province. People were queuing to enter grocery stores, and panic buying had begun, leaving shelves bare. People were fighting, and there was a lot of fearmongering as we all tried to deal with the situation. These were strange times, and strangely, this was and still is our new normal for now. At this point, no one has the virus under control, but more people are testing positive and dying every day.

The terms 'self-isolation' and 'social distancing' are now commonly used. Every day, I have been reminded of those words. When I went for a walk, the streets were strangely empty. I was perplexed as to what was going on. I thought such things only happened in movies. However, this was the new movie, COVID-19.

When I walked past grocery stores, I noticed people clinging to their shopping carts as if they were never going to shop again; they were just waiting to get into the store and shop until there were no more products for others. The most popular items were toilet paper, paper towels, and soap. These were the goods.

At times, the shelves were bare. We were repeatedly told not to panic buy because there was enough food supply to go around. I suppose it's human instinct to do the opposite of what they are told when a pandemic strikes. Social distancing was still emphasized, and we were now told to stay at home unless it was necessary to go out.

However, we were still not on total lockdown in Canada. We could still go for a walk, but we were reminded to stay alert and continue to practice social distancing. As time passed, those were the most frequently used words in the vocabulary. The world was now in a panic, and the future seems uncertain. The devastation of nations and industries will be difficult to comprehend. Many people will be in pain for months, if not years, during this time. It was not a pretty picture as I watched the numbers of cases rise in Canada and around the world, it is difficult to digest.

March 18, 2020

I awoke this morning with a menstrual migraine, and I awoke yesterday with the same migraine and did not feel good. Even though I am not having a period, I am still getting migraines. Today I got some brown spotting. The last time I saw brown spotting was on February 7, and it lasted three days.

Perimenopause is a never-ending story. It's as if I'm having period symptoms without a real menstrual cycle. I know I won't be in menopause until I've gone a year without spotting or a period. I know I'm going through something; my body is changing daily, and I'm not always happy about it.

For a short time, it appeared that I had a break and wasn't having as many hot flashes. When those days happened, my world looked great. I started wondering if it's because I overanalyze the whole perimenopause thing at times. However, my hot flashes have returned and appear to be in overdrive these last few days.

In addition to my migraine from yesterday, I woke up with no energy to do anything. I'm feeling down and have little motivation to do anything. Sorry, but turning fifty has not been a magical experience for me thus far. But who said it would be? Fifty isn't the new forty for me.

On the plus side, my ferritin levels appear to have improved slightly now that I'm back on iron supplements. My doctor has instructed me to continue taking the iron supplement and to have my blood tested again in two months, which I will do. I'm also trying to eat more green vegetables. I adore spinach, and one of my favorite ways to consume it is in the form of a smoothie.

My problem is that I am not particularly adventurous when it comes to food. I tend to stick to what I'm familiar with. I'm not one to embrace change or experiment with new foods. Nonetheless, if you do not try something, you will never know how it tastes. Today I'll have a spinach and fruit shake.

March 19, 2020

A small amount of blood appeared today. Is this a sign that I'm going to be having a light period for the next few days? I hope not, but I don't know for sure.

Fortunately, I have some tampons and pads on hand because I never know what my menstrual cycle will be like or when it will appear. Prior to all this upheaval, my monthlies were very consistent and regular. But now I'm just not sure where I am, especially with my ever-changing body. I have no idea what's going on right now. I'm still suffering from a migraine, but I'll just get on with my day. I'd rather deal with the migraine and hope it goes away soon. If it gets too much, I will take a pill for relief.

I'm not going too far these days because we're in the grip of a pandemic, but I still need to get outside and breathe in some fresh air.

I thought the pleasures of reaching fifty was a milestone, fifty and fantastic, maybe not in my opinion. That is not the case today. Today, I am just fifty years old and stunned. Some days, all I want to do is go back a few years and lie on a beach in the Mediterranean, forgetting about everything, including my age. I don't like getting old.

March 22, 2020

The week of March 22 was a disaster. In addition to recent events, like the COVID-19 pandemic, my desire for sugar seemed to have increased, as did the need for sweet foods. I thought I was over those cravings by this point. I was dealing with everything else. Every time I see chocolate, I can't seem to walk past a store without purchasing something. I am so weak at times, and chocolate has always been one of my weaknesses.

Nonetheless, in my current situation, I am aware that it is only a treat, and that I must exercise caution. I adore British chocolate, which is only available in a few stores in Canada, so it's always a treat and an excuse to visit. My week has been an emotional roller-coaster with this change.

This week, I have seen yet again an increase in the number of hot flashes. Perhaps they were caused by my consumption of coffee, red wine, and sweets, though I am not a heavy drinker. My husband enjoys a glass of red wine now and then. I usually join him when there is a special occasion.

March 23, 2020

A new week has begun, and I will do my best this week to stay busy while also being much more mindful of what I put into my mouth and limiting that dreadful word, sugar. The issue is that sugar is present in everything we consume. Moving forward, I'll just try to be reasonable. It always tastes good at the moment, but it makes me feel bad afterwards. Despite all these years, I sometimes feel like I still have no control over my sugar addiction. Only now things are very different from when I was younger.

When I take a shower, I notice that my muffin top has expanded and that I have gained some weight, which is most likely due to my continued consumption of unnecessary sugar. Not only do I dislike what I see, but I also do not feel well.

Feeling good is far more important than how I appear visually. When I gain these extra pounds, I can feel it, and I get angry at myself for not being in control and fighting my junk food cravings. I know there are healthier options; I just need to think about them more and stop believing I have no control over junk. How heartbreaking is that? Get a hold of yourself, girl, just get a hold of yourself. I might be able to once the current situation has passed.

March 24, 2020

The coronavirus hit the world like nothing else I'd ever seen, and it is not looking pretty. Today I took a walk because I needed to get out of the house and get some fresh air. The streets were strangely quiet and deserted. I walked past the supermarket and saw people still lining up to get in. I walked by and just observed.

I was completely aware of my surroundings while out on my walk, doing my part to practice social distancing. But I was doing it for my own and others' safety. Simply listening to what the health officers were saying. During the pandemic, a chief medical officer echoed those words. He is telling us all to stay at home, be safe, and look after one another.

When I went for my walk, I mostly saw people listening and keeping their distance. I also noticed that stores had been paying attention, at least those that were still open for us to get what we needed. They had begun to place markers in the store to encourage social distancing. For the most part, this worked well; we stood behind the lines and kept our distance from one another. It was insane.

At 11 a.m. every day, or so, our prime minister, Justin Trudeau, would speak and update Canadians on the situation. He'd tell us that assistance was on its way and that the government was there to help.

Although I have been paying attention, it is difficult to stay tuned in and hear the same repetitive story that has been making headlines for the last two weeks. Today, I decided not to get caught up in listening and instead focus on my food preparation, Italian studies, and a little reading.

I will eventually connect with people through the usual social media channels. To be honest, I am not that savvy and do not want to be engaged through those channels all the time. To some extent, I am isolated from others. I see new people every day who have tested positive for the virus. The virus has no regard for age, gender, ethnicity, or social status. It all comes down to taking precautions.

Although I see the world is going through a difficult time, I think of all the frontline healthcare professionals, doctors, nurses, and workers in general who are still working so that we can have the necessities. I salute these people, and whenever I feel down, I remind myself, "Come on, you don't have it so bad. Look what these dedicated people are having to deal with right now."

Now is the time to take a breather from our busy and hectic lifestyles and take a moment.

Myself, I wouldn't say I enjoy cooking, but now that I have more time, I can look up recipes on YouTube and prepare a variety of meals for my husband. The emphasis is no longer on finding work. Who is hiring a fifty-year-old during this pandemic? I had no luck up until this point, and now I might as well forget it.

In fact, I just read an article this morning that talks about age discrimination, which pretty much sums up what I'm saying. On the bright side of things, the weather is getting warmer, and the days are getting longer, which is something to look forward to. Who knows, we might be on full lockdown next week and I won't be able to walk anywhere if that happens.

March 28, 2020

Every day, more and more depressing news arrives. More lives have been lost, and I can only think of the heroic efforts of all health workers, doctors, nurses, and anyone else in that field who is dealing with all of this. Then there are the grocery store employees and pharmacy employees. They are all working extremely hard to ensure that we can all function and have what we require. I am extremely grateful to each one of them.

Every day, new stories of kindness and compassion emerge. At the same time, just watching it day in and day out makes me sad. It seems there are also those trying to exploit the current situation. When hand sanitizer and wipes become commodities, and people try to profit from them. What a disgrace those greedy stores.

When an upscale grocery store in Toronto tried to sell wipes for $30 Canadian, they were called out on social media. The store claimed it was an honest mistake caused by the high demand. Yes, we understand. They immediately halted their tweets and apologized. They should be ashamed. Yes, they should be ashamed.

I walked into a store where hand sanitizer was sixteen dollars and ninety-nine cents, which was outrageous. When I confronted the owner, he mentioned wholesale prices. What utter nonsense. He was referring to selfishness as well as the exploitation of vulnerable people. This was all disgusting and shameful to witness during these times. The province's premier had to step in and tell these profiteering stores that there would be consequences for their actions. *There should no doubt be,* I thought.

Today, I'm just going with the flow. That's all I can say. Every day at 11 o'clock, I watch the prime minister address the nation. I feel like we're in a war, and all I want to know is when it'll be over. But there is no evidence of this yet.

I'm wondering if all this stress and restricted living is exacerbating my hot flashes. They appear to be present throughout the day. I'm back to drinking more caffeinated beverages. It's probably because I'm staying indoors more and have more time. But this is the new normal, not just for me, but for the rest of the world. I'm all over the place mentally.

Some mornings, I really don't want to get out of bed. I try to shake myself out of this unhappy state of mind. But to be honest, it's not easy. I then attempt to alter my mindset.

I think of all those who are sacrificing and saving lives as I am forced to stay indoors for my own and other people's safety. It's not asking too much. All I must do is try to see the light at the end of the tunnel. We haven't even seen the worst yet in Canada. With all my husband's family in the south of Italy, it's frightening to see how quickly the north of Italy exploded, with approximately ten thousand dead as of March 28. This is increasing. It's a heartbreaking reality.

April 4, 2020
We are now in April, and the world is still paralyzed by the ever-expanding pandemic. These days its common to hear discussions about the economy, unemployment, and new regulations. Hashtags are always popular. #Stayhome, #Socialdistancing, #coronavirus.

In the midst of all this craziness, people are still refusing to listen to our healthcare professionals. When the professionals speak, they inform the public that this is a serious problem that must be addressed. People are dying by the minute, which is not a nice thing.

In my hometown of Toronto, we still have some liberties, such as going for a walk while keeping a safe distance to help contain the spread of this virus. We are advised to go grocery shopping once a week. Parks and parking lots have been closed off, so people do not congregate. People were showing defiance and removing any obstructions that have been put in place. The cordons were set up, so people did not gather in large groups. Maybe a 5k fine will wake people up for not obeying the law.

Our numbers in Canada are growing by the day, including residents of the retirement homes and staff. The constant bombardment of all of this is quite depressing if you let it take over your brain. So, while I like to stay informed, I frequently need to divert my attention elsewhere.

During this time, I'm finding YouTube to be a great source of distraction. I love watching the cruise ships and traveling the world from my sofa. I realize there is a beautiful world out there, and one day, things will hopefully get back to normal with some cost.

On the flip side, I am seeing the horror stories play out for passengers stranded on some of the cruise ships. Countries will not let ships dock due to the outbreak, keeping passengers onboard for a month. I hope the cruise industry will bounce back bigger and stronger, as I still want to fulfill my dream of an around-the-world cruise when I retire.

Although now I do not see a rainbow and things are so uncertain, there will be light at the end of this pandemic, I am sure. Although when I go outside, it is weird and eerie to see the streets and watch line-ups at the grocery store. The streets are somewhat empty, apart from the odd person getting in their social distance walk.

It was Saturday, and we needed to go grocery shopping; shopping now appears to be very different from what it used to be. After returning from our weekly grocery shop, I continued to see the long lines at the grocery stores. People standing 2 meters apart, as per the markings placed down on the ground by the store, some wear their masks and gloves, while others do not.

I just have never seen anything like it. But I am trying to keep my spirits. I feel good right now and I have a roof and food in my house. I am blessed. There are plenty of people in much more of a dire situation than mine. The best thing right now is to listen to the professionals and stay home. This is the right thing to do.

I continue to see that lots of health professionals are risking their own lives for us. Some of them are losing their own battle with the virus. These people are true heroes, doing their jobs day in and day out during these trying times.

Meanwhile, in Italy, the numbers are astounding. 13,000 people and counting have died in Italy, and it breaks my heart to watch the numbers each day. Fortunately, those numbers have not yet creeped too far into the south, but each day it is more and more scary to watch.

As the United States struggles to gain control of the situation, New York is seeing many people die, and it is all too much. There are leaders talking worldwide about the lack of masks, ventilators, and clothing for health professionals. I find this a little ridiculous. I still feel as if I am living in a movie.

The news is still consumed by the coronavirus; all kinds of stories are happening around the world.

The numbers released for Toronto were not good, and they are saying the next two weeks will be critical in this battle. The numbers will be lower if more people listen and stay home. Yes, people stay home. Do not leave the house unless necessary. You can get some air but keep your distance. Why can't humans get it sometimes?

April 8, 2020

Today was not a good day; I think I ate something the day before and my stomach reacted. I spent the whole day in bed with practically no energy and a bad headache. My hot flashes were in full swing, so they did not help my situation. Of course, with what's happening around us, I became a little paranoid because of COVID, which continues to take multiple lives and there is no certainty regarding the virus.

Vaccines and research are still in the making as scientists and doctors are learning more about this virus. I even saw something that said a bad migraine and a lack of energy are related. My mind and thoughts are scattered at this point, as is the rest of the world. I started to think I may have COVID. I think reading that did not help, but got me thinking: do I have it?

I feel these are dark and scary times right now. Although I am in a better situation than some people and should not complain, I think it is all too much for anyone. At least, I have my husband close by. I know some people are totally isolated from others.

April 10, 2020

Today is supposed to be a holiday, but instead the world is urged to stay home. The numbers continue to climb and now, worldwide, there are 1.5 million known cases of COVID-19. Worldwide, to date, there have been 100,000 deaths from the virus. It could be months or years before they develop a vaccine for this virus, as it is still evolving. Researchers, doctors, and scientists are all doing their part to find a cure.

As of today, the United States is the leading country in the number of cases of the virus and it looks like it will soon surpass Italy in the number of deaths. It's just so heartbreaking to watch the world change from how we knew it.

There are so many stories of heroism and heartfelt caring. I read some stories or listen to heartbroken families, and it brings tears to my eyes. I feel sad, so very sad.

It is the start of the Easter weekend. For sure, this one will be different. Health professionals and leaders have urged Canadians to stay at home and have a staycation anywhere in the nation. You should not go and see family members or, for that fact, hold any gatherings other than in your home with the people that you live with at this time. We have been told to keep our interactions to FaceTime, messaging, WhatsApp, Skype, or Zoom.

This new virtual way of connecting is all for our safety and to protect all those brave heroes fighting to save lives. I realize this pandemic is a serious thing. Enforcement officers will be out in the city this weekend to ensure people are not doing what they should not be doing. That applies to anyone not respecting our new physical distancing measures put in place to combat this virus.

I have come to accept this as the new normal. After all, there is nothing else one can do. In the last few weeks, though, I have not been sleeping well. That is nothing new to me. My hot flashes are still there, like a bad cold that will never go away. When I think of the current situation, my anxiety levels start to rise. I find that if I tune into the news too much, I start thinking that I have COVID-19, which causes me to panic and feel like I can't breathe. Yes, it is too much.

I try to connect with people through messenger, WhatsApp, or by phone. The topic of conversation is dominated by this pandemic and the current situation and nothing more. Our conversations are about the state of the world, the number of deaths, the good people are doing, and the sacrificing. Other topics are how we are trying to stay busy.

Well, my exercise routine has gone out the window. I will take an occasional walk, and for now, my YouTube shows allow me to escape. I am still trying to improve my Italian and love watching Italian TV.

April 13, 2020

Yesterday was Easter Sunday and it will be an Easter remembered by the current worldwide lockdown due to COVID 19. The pope delivered a mass with no congregation, and Andrea Bocelli performed some music from an empty duomo in Milan. Different scenes, I am sure, were seen throughout the world.

As we continue to practice social distancing in Toronto, the enforcement police remain vigilant for those few who prefer to ignore the law and not do the right thing. But I guess they will have to face the consequences with a fine if they refuse to listen.

For the most part, we are doing well in Toronto and our numbers remain on the lower side. Having said that, numbers continue to grow. The world has 1.8 million cases and there have been 115,000 deaths globally thus far. This number is constantly changing and on the rise. On the flip side of all this, some countries are seeing a drop and are even relaxing restrictions. I know the urge is to get things back to normal, especially the economy.

Toronto will continue its state of emergency for another 28 days. I am happy to do that; I am sort of getting used to this now, being in our 5th week. I say let it all play out if it needs to be. But I hope we just get a grip on things and do not let our guard down too soon.

My days seem the same now, and I continue to wake up early and endure my sleepless nights. My husband continues to work because where he is working is an essential service. He wakes early every morning, and I am awake with him, even if I only got two hours of sleep the night before. This morning I went back to bed, as I often have for the last four weeks.

At five in the morning, I am back in bed; I am not even sleeping, just thinking about the current situation. When I wake up, I just feel tired, and I must drag myself out of bed. Today was another one of those days where I could not be bothered. It was rainy outside. I decided I would just stay on the couch and spend yet another day surfing the TV. Although most news channels only cover the coronavirus as the main story, almost 2 months later.

April 15, 2020

Today was another trying day. I had to struggle out of bed. But I did it in the end. Yesterday, for some reason, I had more energy than today. It's supposed to snow in the afternoon, but it feels like minus five outside. You'd think I'd be used to the Canadian weather by now. We should be 10° warmer than we are right now.

However, April and even May can be unpredictable. We're getting closer to spring and summer, which is always a good thing. Schools will not reopen on May 4, and we will have to wait and see which way the COVID curve moves. The curve is being discussed by every expert.

Places like the United States and Europe are currently at their peak. Canada is not there yet, and we should not relax our guard in this situation. The economy is the topic of the day. We're finally getting a sense of how different industries are faring and how they're being affected by it all. Some industries, such as the food supply chain, online shopping, and healthcare, are still doing well. Grocery stores, pharmacies and healthcare workers continue to be our heroes, risking everything every day to save lives and do their best amid the chaos.

I know I need to limit the amount of news I watch each day and try to find other outlets to focus on. At times, it's mentally taxing for me to watch. I am loving watching my Italian TV right now, and I am sometimes motivated by my YouTube fitness shows. I would rather get a bit of fresh air, though, when the nicer weather arrives.

The pandemic's ever-changing numbers continue to astound the world. They are shocking, and the number of new cases worldwide is quickly approaching 2 million. Some countries have eased restrictions, while others have not. For my part, I would rather endure this new way of life. When the time comes to lift restrictions, it should be a methodical operation and a departure from how things were previously.

As I was reading the British newspaper, I learned that a nurse died of coronavirus today, but she had just delivered a baby. I'm crying as I read this. All of this is very real. I then read stories of hope, such as how a 106-year-old was recovering from the virus and was about to be discharged from the hospital.

Then there was the 99-year-old World War II veteran who was walking to raise funds for the British National Health Service. He has now raised ten million dollars. He is walking up and down with his walker and will continue to do so if donations keep coming in. That is truly amazing, and I applaud him. God bless him; he deserves a medal for his efforts. What an incredible story. Many people around the world are doing amazing things to make doctors', health workers', and frontline workers' lives easier. These people are incredible, putting their lives and families at risk to help during the pandemic.

April 17, 2020

We are almost at the end of our 5th week of lockdown in Toronto. Although, I do not know if I should use that term here. In Italy, lockdown means no venturing out whatsoever and only one person can do the grocery shopping. They cannot even go in their cars or for a walk. We still have the privilege of walking. Although their numbers are on the decline, there is still vigilance.

Meanwhile, on the other side of the Canadian border, the U.S. wants to see the economy gradually return to work in stages. It states that if they have low numbers, it may reopen sooner for some, like the first of May or prior. The figures are rising in Canada, as they are globally. Long-term care has been thrust into the spotlight across the world.

When you read some of the stories, many of the elderly and vulnerable are not being well cared for.

The problem is that workers are becoming infected as well, and in some cases, there aren't enough people to man the sites. In these trying times, who can blame people for not wanting to work in a place where they may be put in danger?

I've lost all motivation at home, and I'm finding it difficult. All of this, combined with perimenopause and how I feel, is my worst nightmare. I haven't been this emotional in a long time, but with all the recent events, I'm feeling sadder and more up and down. At this time of year, we usually have warmer weather, lighter nights, and the birds begin to sing. It's that time of year when you tell yourself, "I want to lose ten pounds so I can enjoy the summer."

2020 will be a different year, one can only wait and see. Will we be able to enjoy the nice weather and get around? It's all just waiting to see how it all plays out right now. It looks like learning for schools and universities is out for now. Although there was talk about May 4, that date has changed. I guess for now, online and virtual schooling is the way to go. Having talked to friends, it has already had implications in Ontario, as occupying kids is not easy.

April 18, 2020

I didn't watch or listen to the news today. I must say that not having to hear anything makes me feel better. I'm starting to believe I'm sick, as I had a conversation with my girlfriend today, who stated that she had a cough, sore throat, and a slight fever one day. She thinks she has

COVID-19 and has decided to stay inside. I told her that I believe it is taking a toll on all of us mentally and emotionally because it is so draining. I advised her to avoid news and other outlets, including the internet and social media, to give her brain a rest.

My back, neck, and everything else hurts today. I feel my age and more. I'm starting over with my paranoid thoughts; am I getting sick? I sincerely hope not. When we go out, I make every effort to keep my physical distance. It is difficult, however, when others are not as committed as I believe I am. It's like a zoo in the grocery store; no one is paying attention. I'm doing everything I can to avoid them. The store appears to only have the cash set up at a distance, but you can let loose as usual inside. It irritates me.

Next week, I need to try to establish an improved routine. I'm being hard on myself, and I'm aware that I've gained some weight in the last five weeks. It's not easy; I'm sure the rest of the world feels the same way. I'm hoping for a better day tomorrow. My mood is fluctuating these days and hot flashes are still ever present. Then I have emotional days when I read about people dying or see heartbreaking stories of true bravery, it is so hard to watch.

My sleep is another story, and I can't say I've slept well in a long time. My sleep has gotten even worse during this COVID-19 period. I couldn't sleep at first, but I convinced myself it was because of the caffeine. I tried going without caffeine for a day, but I still couldn't sleep. The sheets are on throughout the night, and I push them off and pull them back on. My story never changes. Tossing and turning, I have come to accept that sleep is not my friend and will never be something I can ease into. It is very annoying not to have a good night's sleep.

The COVID-19 numbers are changing daily. I will try and keep the weekends free of any kind of news. It's not that I do not want to know the latest that's going on, because I do. However, I can only take it in small doses. I am exhausted.

April 29, 2020

I just returned from my daily walk, and even though we are approaching the end of April, it is still chilly, and I am wearing gloves and a hood today. I know the month of April can be a mixed bag of weather in Canada. You never know how things will turn out. It had even snowed earlier in the month.

For many years, April was a month of fundraising for M.S. (Multiple Sclerosis) and walking for that cause in the Niagara region. On the day of the walk, you never knew what the weather would be like. One year it was in the heat with sunshine, and the next was like a whirlwind from the Wizard of Oz. But that was all in the past. I had forgotten how things used to be. Back to the present, we are now in our seventh week of lockdown.

We are learning new behaviors, but there is still much to be thankful for. We can leave our houses without being questioned. That is not the case in other parts of the world, which, as I previously stated, are under total lockdown. Although our government and leaders are closely monitoring the situation, they are not ready to relax the current restrictions. Well, at least not in Ontario, which is the province where I reside.

I have to say, as much as these times restrict my behavior, I would rather be safe than sorry. I am alive and breathing right now. The numbers are astounding, and I cannot even begin to imagine the pain experienced by all the families that have suffered the loss of a loved one in this pandemic. The media and health officials are talking globally in terms of numbers. These numbers are heart-wrenching, and they are people. Everyday people, including the frontline heroes, who are trying to save the lives of others.

At present, there have been more than three million cases worldwide and over two hundred thousand deaths, and the number is climbing. The United States, along with Europe, has taken the brunt of the damage. Fifty-six thousand lives have been lost to date, and this number is still rising.

Despite the grim statistics, there is some cause for optimism. As we all watched, Italy, which was hit hard at first, is relaxing some of its restrictions as the number of cases decreases. Parts of the United States are also reopening, and it appears that everyone just wants to get the economy moving again. Other provinces in Canada are following suit.

However, each province has its own plan. Quebec has been harder hit than Ontario, and they will gradually reopen certain sectors and schools. Personally, I prefer the slower and safer approach. Ontario school systems will not reopen for another month.

Although our leaders have discussed the framework for reopening, no dates have been set. Dates will be set as medical professionals see fit, and there will be a gradual flattening of the curve and a drop in numbers for consecutive weeks. We're looking at another five weeks of this. That is OK if we can see light at the end of the tunnel. It is going to take a while for a vaccine to be created.

My doctor had sent me another requisition to go and get blood work done. But I will just hold off for now and hope I am doing well. I have started to take my iron tablets, so we will see. I have not seen any spotting since mid-March. But I am at the stage now where I never know, so I guess I should not get too excited.

Many people are now working from home. This is the new virtual reality of how things are done now. With millions laid off due to the pandemic, they are joining a club of people who were already in that position. I am grateful for small things now, and I am unable to complain about the situation.

This pandemic, I believe, is a wake-up call for us all to examine and reflect on how we take life and things for granted. What was the world and life like before? When people were running around like headless chickens, thinking to themselves, "Oh, I'm so busy." The only thing you could hear was, "Oh, I'm so busy, busy, busy."

We humans like to be busy, and now we have all this free time. Parents were too preoccupied with the busyness of life. Their children were occupied with activities. Driving around town was a chore. A short drive would take an eternity if there were cars on the road and traffic was bad.

Nowadays, with less traffic on the roads, we can breathe a little easier and there is less pollution. We're not really driving much these days. People are mostly staying at home. We are surviving without all the luxuries and things to which we've grown accustomed. We were shopping for clothes, designer bags, shoes, and other indulgences. Getting your nails and hair done, maybe even getting a massage if you needed one, and going to the dentist, which I know I haven't done in a long time.

All these little pastimes we used to enjoy are no longer commonplace. At least in my hometown of Toronto, these establishments are currently closed, and who knows when they will reopen and thrive again?

I know that when everything reopens, it will take some time to get back to normal. To put a positive spin on the situation, parents can now spend more time with their children. More downtime and rest are possible now, which is always a good thing. We can show so much love, respect, and appreciation to our doctors, nurses, caregivers, essential workers, grocery clerks, and all those who help the less fortunate during these difficult times.

May 1, 2020

We have entered a new month and still the pandemic is with us. March seemed to last forever and now we are in May. Countries all over the globe are now attempting to develop a cure or vaccine to alleviate the situation. That could be a long way off. However, there is some hope in my city of Toronto, where guidelines are being recommended for businesses when they reopen. Although there is no set date, that is positive news.

All this time spent inside has not been good for my waistline. On some days, I continue to struggle with the food I eat. At times, I feel like I'm overdoing it on the sugar, but it's my only source of happiness and enjoyment during this period of time.

Today, I listened to our Premier of Ontario's one-hour briefing. Now, I don't like listening every day, but it appears that the optimism I mentioned is correct. Several businesses could reopen on May 4 with guidelines. Businesses that can maintain a physical distance, as this is our new norm for the time being. They included garden centers, construction companies, and other businesses that only offered curbside pickup and no in-store shopping. Retailers, personal care stores, and offices have not been included in this category, nor have schools, restaurants, concerts, or sporting events.

This is a gradual process, as we and the rest of the world deal with the pandemic. But at least we're heading in the right direction.

All of this is having an impact on my mental health, it is not easy. I'm trying not to get too involved in things. I try to just get on with it, knowing that we must all emerge stronger and wiser.

In time, we will view this as a period where we all slowed down and took the opportunity to reflect. I even made sugar-free banana bread, which was delicious. The challenge is trying not to sit so much, but I think I'm doing OK for now. I've also tried a few home fitness video workouts. Despite the lack of consistency, it is a start.

May 5, 2020

We are now into the eighth week of our new normal. That is social distancing, staying home and staying safe. I only go out once a day when my body makes it. I walk for an hour or so and come straight back home. My outdoor exercise and my life for the past eight weeks continues as I try to escape with my travel TV and cruise shows. I need to go somewhere, even if it is while sitting on my sofa.

For now, it is best to stay close to home and wait for the green light from our health and government officials. They continue to lead, and I have confidence in what they are saying despite their critics.

Meanwhile, in the U.S., many state beaches and other necessary businesses have started to reopen. From what I see on the news, there are crowded places. The death toll in the U.S. has now reached 71,000 and is still on the rise. Future predictions are not looking good, and it is difficult to watch it all unfold. You also have protesters demanding the economy be reopened, oblivious to what is going on.

On the other hand, everyone has their own right to express their opinions. There will be an election in November and all eyes, I am sure, will be looking to see how it all plays out.

Meanwhile, as the death rate in the U.K surpasses that of Italy, some places, including various provinces in Canada, have begun to gradually open with guidelines. I can't emphasize enough how much I prefer a slow approach that prioritizes people's health. I understand that economies and people are suffering, but caution is essential.

We currently have no cure, no vaccine, and have no idea where this is all going. I just try to take each day as it comes. I'm still only able to handle what's going on in small doses. It's too difficult to watch every day. This is already the eighth week. People are itching to get out and return to normal living as the weather changes and the nights become lighter. I still believe that sacrifice is preferable to a new wave.

Even if it means getting excited about going for a daily walk or going to the grocery store once a week, I appear to have adapted to this new normal.

Hopefully, as our cases decline, we will hear more encouraging news in Canada in the coming weeks. This is what needs to happen before officials and health experts feel comfortable moving forward. I will continue to pray and think about all the frontline workers around the world, as well as those who have died while fighting this pandemic. These people are heroes, and they should all be recognized for their efforts to keep us safe.

I'm still dealing with perimenopause, and I'm getting no sleep. I wish I knew what it was like to sleep six, let alone eight hours. I used to think it was the caffeine and hot flashes that kept me awake, but now I'm not so sure. I was still having trouble sleeping three days after finishing my caffeine-free detox. With what is going on right now, there are likely many factors at play, which isn't helping.

I appear to be waking up drenched and wet, but this is nothing new. Hot flashes, mood swings, and at times feelings of sadness are all part of the fifty-year-old experience. I'm relieved that I'm not alone and that I can discuss my symptoms and the ongoing sagas of being a woman with other women in my life. I hoped I'd have had more education and forewarning as I approached the age of fifty. People just laugh and make fun of that age, which is not nice. I wish I really knew what to expect. No one talks about it, and there is no script for what is to come.

May 11, 2020

We are now in the ninth week of the lockdown, and we are about to see a limited, gradual reopening of businesses. Things will not be the same for people anytime soon. It feels like a nightmare to me. Now I'm numb to the situation and just keep going. In all honesty, that is what must be done. Just keep going and be grateful for any small improvement.

A positive change is always a good thing. I'm even at the point where I'm willing to wait. Hoping there isn't a second wave, which is almost certainly unavoidable when all is said and done. I can't believe the topic of discussion and what has dominated my own conversations and news, which is the global pandemic. The COVID-19 virus is still wreaking havoc around the world, paralyzing travel, the economy, and our always busy, busy lives.

Some parts of the world continue to move faster in their approach to reopening; they want to get their economy moving. Some are more cautious, and I keep hearing nine weeks in, more testing, more testing, more testing. I am also hearing there is not enough PPE (personal protective equipment) to go around, whereas health workers are being reassured there is enough. To be honest, at times, I find it difficult to find a mask.

Usually, I try to keep my exercise to once a day, and since it is in the early morning, I do not wear a mask. Especially since I practice social distancing and there are usually only a few people around. That may change this week in Toronto with more businesses slowly opening and there may be more people out and about. When I do go to the grocery store, I put my mask on and try to distance myself.

I am still taking precautions and taking this seriously. The thing is, when you are in the grocery store, people are getting close, and it seems like they are not even paying attention. At least if they are wearing a mask and I am wearing mine, I feel a bit protected. I am a lot more aware now than when this all began.

At first, I thought I was going to get sick or start to feel anxious. I think that is because I was overwhelmed with it all. Now I try not to focus on it too much and just get on with it. It seems like our state of emergency will be extended until June 2. Health professionals are looking to see consistency in our numbers, and we need to see a two-week downward peak first before we move forward. I say whatever it takes, I am with the health and medical officers. I have confidence in them.

Meanwhile, I continue to deal with my hot flashes on a daily and nightly basis. They are really driving me mad. In the heat of the moment, I am sweating. I mean, soaking wet. What is up with that?

It is just ongoing. I forgot I was on the change because there is so much going on with all this COVID stuff. I forgot I was perimenopausal. I've been almost two months without a menstrual period of any kind. I know that the body can change, and I may get a monthly. I just never know when, but I am happy that nothing is happening.

With age comes the continued aches and pains. My joints seem to seize up at times, and I am starting to get paranoid that I am getting arthritis in my hands. My mother has rheumatoid arthritis and is on medication. I have my days where I feel some aches in my fingers and hands. Isn't ageing great?

It is all about one's health and nothing more. It is exhausting sometimes. I've realized that I can't eat like I used to. Trying to explain that to someone who is in the grip of a pandemic and wants to eat the fridge is hard. I am trying to eliminate some of my sugar intake now. I have to say I was proud of my recent detox, but I always feel I need a treat on the weekend. Then I think that I should be able to have a treat, and I should not always be so hard on myself.

For years, I fought the sugar war, probably along with half of the population. I was mentally struggling and, at times, losing control as I continued to eat mindlessly. At fifty, I thought I needed to pay more attention.

May 20, 2020

We've reached week ten of our new normal. I've had to drag myself out of bed for the past two days. I simply do not have the motivation to get out of bed. Maybe, with everything going on, that's part of the reason. The subject of COVID-19 continues to dominate the news, albeit with different headlines.

With over four million cases worldwide and counting, it remains a terrible time in our history. Nations are still working to develop a vaccine, which will take some time. I'm at a loss for words these days. I'm just existing during it all. I'm trying hard not to feel down, but some days it's just not possible. I simply cannot be bothered.

Sometimes when I indulge, I continue to argue with myself about what I eat. Once I feel my midsection, I get angry with myself. I have the impression that I sit far too much. I did, however, get in an hour and a half of social distancing walking this morning. The entire outdoor scene, including streets, people, and everything, seems strange. When I walk, I wear my headphones and listen to music to keep me moving. I just walk until I reach my daily time and then stop. I walk and notice how beautiful and green it is. The sky is blue, and the trees are bright and full of buds right now.

The weather for the next few days looks sunny and bright with warmer temperatures, which makes me feel a bit better. At the same time, I am not happy, and I am no longer free. Life has changed in recent months, and not for the better. Things are just so bad; I know I'm not alone. The entire world is living in this manner at the same time. As countries have begun to relax some restrictions, different places are doing what their leaders believe is best. I will continue to receive updates, but only in small amounts.

Toronto has entered stage one, allowing more businesses and non-essential businesses to open. Even though some restrictions have been lifted, I am not in the mood to go out and be around people. I am hesitant and see that there is no rush.

The cases remain in Toronto, and we cannot relax our guard until we see the numbers decrease. Health officials now advise us to wear masks when we are unable to physically distance ourselves. If we are in close quarters, we can also use a scarf or some other type of face covering. In Toronto, masks are not mandatory right now. Parks, golf courses, and other spectator-free sports can also be resumed in Toronto. National sports, concerts, and other large gatherings will have to wait. That makes sense, in my opinion.

Our own human behavior will have a major impact on all of this. Some people will do as they are told, while others will refuse. They will try to take a seat in an area that has been cordoned off for a reason. Ignorance gets a hold of some people first before safety and common sense. As the city of Toronto remains in a state of emergency, we will have to wait until around June 2 to see what will happen.

At this point, I am just going with what the officials and leaders are saying. I still trust and confide in their decisions about the people of our province. This summer will look somewhat different as people are itching to get out and about now with the warmer weather. The weather has been a long time coming, and I hope things will only get better.

My husband and I usually enjoy traveling once or twice a year. Fortunately, this year we did not book any travel. Unlike our friends, who love concerts and have some travel booked. It seems these companies and airlines are giving credits or rescheduling for upcoming events, even though there are no given dates. To some degree, the situation is like it was ten weeks ago.

There are still businesses that are not open yet and will take time to open. Many guidelines will be needed for all sectors and industries in the constantly changing new normal. In fact, each day brings new developments. Today I am hearing about lots of companies going into bankruptcy, which is sad. Then there are the thousands of workers who have been laid off. This is the result of the pandemic.

May 27, 2020

We are now in our eleventh week of adjusting to the new normal, but, like the rest of the world, I just keep going because I must. I've accepted that this will be the norm for the foreseeable future. I still have days when getting out of bed is easy and other days that are a struggle. We've had some nice hot, humid weather here in Toronto for the last week, and after being cooped up for so long, people just want to get out. That is understandable. I was able to get up and out of bed today before the heat set in.

Seeing people wearing masks is very strange. I can't help but notice that bus drivers and car drivers are wearing masks as they pass me by. The buses remain empty. Few people use public transportation these days. I haven't taken a bus or the Toronto subway in nearly three months. Right now, I only walk when I need to. If I go for my early morning walk, I don't have to dodge as much, and I'm always aware of my social distancing. If I must move, I don't mind. People, for the most part, maintain their social distance.

This morning was hot, and my walking route took me partly in the sun and partly in the shade, with a welcome warm wind at times. Halfway through my walk, I decided to stop and enjoy ten minutes of sunshine. I sat by the playground, but there were no children there. The swings, slides, and climbing apparatus are all taped off, which has been the case for months.

The COVID-19 notice is prominent and large enough for everyone to see. I continue my walk after enjoying a few minutes in the sun. I feel disheartened when I look around me. It's simply strange. It shouldn't be after the last three months, but it is. I'm not sure what the summer will be like this year, but it will be different from the last for my husband and me.

A few more locations have opened, as have a few more retailers. I'm not in the mood to go shopping right now. The cases have not improved and the total number of cases in the world has surpassed five million. The United States has lost 100,000 people, and the global toll is rising.

Although Canada is going through its own phase, I've grown numb to it all. It's still exhausting and emotional. I know we'll get through it all, even though it may seem like an endless journey. The world may look and feel different, but we will eventually arrive. Some countries are beginning to welcome tourists again, which is a good sign. The global tourism industry, like many others, has taken a significant hit. Every mode of transportation will look different. My hope is that people gain the confidence to travel again.

After discovering my love of cruising a few years ago, I would be devastated if I could no longer cruise. When this is over, I'll be getting back on a boat. You will not be able to keep me away. Although cruise lines are changing their policies and raising their cleanliness standards, I have heard that if you are diabetic, you may be unable to travel. I hope that's not the case. My husband is diabetic, and if this is true, it will be devastating to our family. The only thing to do now is wait and see how all industries ease back into business when it is safe to do so.

June 3, 2020

As the pandemic continues, we are now in week twelve of our new normal. The city of Toronto has issued a state of emergency until June 30. At that point, health officials and leaders will decide whether more businesses will reopen and whether we can proceed to the next stage. The number of cases appears to be fluctuating right now. I know there was a spike after Mother's Day here, but it appears that people had had enough and needed to get out.

Thousands of people gathered in a downtown neighborhood just over a week ago, disregarding social distancing protocol and some not wearing masks. What do they think we're all sacrificing for? This behavior irritates me greatly. The people of Toronto are doing an excellent job, and there are people who choose not to listen.

A vaccine seems a long way off at this point. No one knows when or how long it will take. All nations are trying to be the first to produce a vaccine. I know COVID-19 is here to stay for a while, and we will have to adapt.

I can't believe it's been thirteen weeks and the numbers from this pandemic are still changing by the minute. There have been over six million cases worldwide, with 380,000 (and counting) deaths. So far, the countries with the most cases are the United States, Brazil, Russia, the United Kingdom, and Spain. This is still going on, and each country has its own set of problems.

These days, I try not to pay too much attention to the news. The last few weeks have been emotionally draining. I'm just doing my best to get through it. My sleep is still poor because my hot flashes are persistent. It's a bit much with this pandemic and my perimenopause struggles at times.

To think we once took simple things for granted. Just like going to my hairdresser, shopping, and walking down the street. I haven't texturized my hair in about three months, and I miss my hairdresser. We don't know when this sector will open in Toronto, and it doesn't appear to be anytime soon. So, for the time being, my husband is my hairdresser. I shaved my hair and put on a wig last week. Yes, thank goodness for wigs. There is always a solution, and this is mine right now.

As I continue to watch the news on occasion, the stories have shifted away from the pandemic dominator. Other headlines are taking over the front pages. The recent death of George Floyd, an African American who was murdered by police in Minneapolis, has dominated the news.

On May 25, 2020, the entire world watched in agony as Mr. Floyd uttered his final words, "I can't breathe." He also yelled for his mother. The officer kneeled for 8 minutes and 46 seconds on his neck. He murdered George Floyd, and witnessing it was heartbreaking and difficult. How can you handcuff someone, lie them face down without a struggle, and then murder them?

Three other officers on duty that day stood by and watched this happen. Bystanders who saw what was happening before their eyes pleaded with the officer to get off him. It was too late; the damage had been done, and it was a disgrace.

For the past few weeks, America's crisis has dominated the news. Protests took place all over the United States and the world. People are outraged and, like me, are struggling to comprehend and digest what was witnessed. One officer has been charged with third-degree murder as well as manslaughter. Is that sufficient? The other three have not yet been charged. The only quick action was to remove them from the force. These are not the officers who serve and protect the public. My hope is that justice is served and that everyone is held accountable.

As the unrest across the border continues, the pandemic and stay-at-home orders remain in effect. Of course, because I am at home, aside from my daily walk, I have time to see all the events.

June 12, 2020

As our province enters the second stage of reopening the economy, we must wait, and soon it will be our turn in Toronto. A few things happened today: gatherings were expanded to groups of up to ten people, with physical separation; provincial parks and beaches are now open; and visitors to nursing homes and group homes with no COVID cases are welcome. Numbers vary depending on the establishment. Globally, the care of the elderly has come under scrutiny.

The situation is constantly changing. Another change is that wearing a mask while riding public transportation in Toronto will now be required. We'll see if more restrictions are lifted by the end of the week. It's all about the figures.

Three months later, we are still in the grip of a pandemic, and things are far from normal. I'm still trying to get a grasp of it all, but it's not easy mentally. I talk to others, and they are all feeling the same way, anxious and unsure of what is going to happen. Nothing appears to be the same. Life can change so quickly. If only I could be in Capo Vaticano, Italy, like I was last year. I seem to have forgotten what it's like to be happy. It just feels like I'm trapped in a bubble with no way out.

June 18, 2020

It's been another crazy week, and Toronto has yet to advance to stage two, as some other cities have. The numbers are looking positive, so we could see more restrictions eased for businesses by the end of the week. I am relieved to see that the numbers are decreasing. Whatever it takes; it's been months of living like this, and I'm not about to go back to my old ways any time soon. If the province continues to open with caution, it will make me feel better.

July 5, 2020

Toronto is now in stage two, and the pandemic continues. I must say that I have nothing but praise for our leaders' slow and cautious steps toward reopening. Looking at the bigger picture of the world and across our borders reveals a significant difference from what is happening in Canada. I'll do my best to maintain my new normal. As we continue to live, I simply accept it all. I'm trying to keep a social distance and not really engage. Caution and human behavior will be essential, as will avoidance of stupidity. Now I am fully conscious and always aware.

As I continue to navigate perimenopause, I continue to have good and bad days. I haven't had a menstrual period in three months, and I'm overjoyed. In fact, I'm about to enter my fourth month. I suppose I shouldn't get too excited based on what I've heard. You can go six months without having a menstrual period from what I understand. We're all different, but for the time being, I'm content. If I can make it to mid-July and reach four months, I'll be on the right track.

My colonoscopy is scheduled for Friday, July 10. This week I've been researching my preparation for this over the internet. The first step is to purchase my prep liquid, which I will need to consume both before and on the day of my colonoscopy. I also need to take some laxatives to get the process started. I'll start eating lighter and changing my diet about three days before. I know I have a polyp, and they will most likely find it and remove it a second time.

Trying to be proactive is at the forefront of my mind at this stage in my life. This procedure does not appeal to me in the least. But who wants to have an instrument inserted up their behind for an examination? I'll begin my prep diet, that will consist of lighter foods such as white bread, rice, liquids, and other uninteresting items.

Who said turning fifty was going to be easy? That stigma that comes with turning fifty. Yes, it is overhyped, but not for the better. I'm continuing to discover that it's all about health and wellness, as well as watching what I eat. Although I am content with my age, some days are better than others. On some days, I feel older than fifty.

Suddenly, I need to get all these milestone health checks and vaccinations or consider getting them. My most recent blood count was normal, and my doctor advised me to reduce my iron supplements for the time being. I'll be re-evaluated in about three months. My iron levels have always fluctuated. I am just trying to keep more on top of the health stuff. I know it will take a lot more effort to keep my looks and just maintain my body now.

Growing up, I was always self-conscious about my body, even though I was never obese. I had an athletic frame and always thought I should look more feminine. My legs were muscular, and I didn't like how they looked. I rarely wore skirts or dresses.

Then, as I grew older, I felt more at ease wearing pants. It wasn't until I reached a certain age that I realized I had a mild case of body dysmorphia, even though I wasn't at the point where I wanted to harm myself. I had a lot of issues with my body image. According to my friends, I had a great body, but I always felt I was overweight and not looking good enough.

Acceptance of myself and learning to love my small package took time. I realized that I didn't have to conform or be overly feminine. I should simply be myself. I remember my mother telling me when I was younger to put on some make-up and eyeliner. As she would say, "Be a little ladylike." Who said I had to be ladylike?

I was never interested in make-up or felt the need to wear make-up. I looked and felt better just the way I was. My girlfriend introduced me to Revlon foundation make-up for my complexion when I was sixteen. When we did go out for a night, I put some on and looked nice with the bright red lipstick I was wearing at the time.

That quickly faded, and I am relieved that I no longer wear make-up. I thought my appearance was just as good without it. I look better *au naturel*. If I want, I can put a little lipstick on and call it a day. I have nothing against women who wear make-up; it's just not for me.

July 10, 2020

I had to prepare for my colonoscopy before the actual procedure day. It all began at the start of the week. I started a light diet on Tuesday to get my body ready for the procedure. I had pasta, white bread, and other recommended light items. I was only permitted to drink liquids, clear liquids, and jello by the time my prep day, Thursday, July 9, rolled around. For lunch, I had chicken broth, and after that, not much else.

Prior to the day of my colonoscopy, I had to get ready for it beforehand. My girlfriend who underwent the same procedure reported that it was not a nice experience. Once I reached fifty, I knew it was something I had to do.

The day before, it wasn't too bad to only have liquids. It was a little difficult for me to digest drinking the preparation potion. The flavor wasn't the nicest, but fortunately I would only be going to my bathroom, the couch, and back there. I got my first round at six p.m. and then spent the next several hours in the bathroom with a foul odor. Fortunately, I was able to sleep a little longer and only got up once to use the restroom.

I drank more amounts of the cleansing potion today, the day of the surgery. Again, I drank and did the bathroom-to-sofa routine at six in the morning. I was out the door and on my way to the clinic by eleven in the morning. All I could think was that I needed to control myself until I reached the clinic.

Fortunately, I was able to do so, and when I got there, I peed. I believe my nerves started to take over and I was unable to leave the restroom. I finally did and went into the clinic. After completing the paperwork, I was led to a different room where I received an IV before being led down to the operating room. What a sweet and gracious surgeon and nurse. My fears vanished as soon as I entered the operating room and I felt at ease.

The anesthesiologist gave me a dose, and the next thing I knew, I was lying on my side and out cold. The sound of the nurse asking me whether I was OK, made me realize I had awakened and was in the recovery room. As she kept an eye on my vital signs, I began to gently awaken. What a relief when I realized, I had come around.

As soon as I felt good, I was able to get dressed and drink an ensure shake. It was all over and not so bad after all. I just get nervous at the thought of procedures. I have only had one other, to remove a polyp some years before and I was an emotional wreck, crying going into that procedure. All being well, I do not have to have another colonoscopy for another ten years.

Despite the ups and downs of perimenopause, it appears my hot flashes are currently not so bad right now. They don't appear to be happening as frequently to me now. I will always embrace these moments. There are occasions, however, when I feel I may simply be overanalyzing them and that it's all in my head. Going through a life shift is strange. I consider myself fortunate to have lived to an advanced age, but I also consider mortality.

Even though I keep trying to eat healthy and exercise frequently, I am aware that it will take more time and work now that I am fifty to reduce the fat and that eating poorly will affect my muffin top. I am no longer able to eat anything I want without worrying about gaining weight because of my age. I constantly struggle and occasionally always feel bad for indulging.

Even though, I do not always eat well. I am aware that occasionally I need to ease up on myself. I tend to be quite critical and harsh. On the other hand, we are still in the pandemic phase and, like everyone, I have my off days where I think I do not care.

As I get older, I have periods when I feel OK and days where I don't. I've noted before that I get aches and pains. Maybe it's how I slept or if I sat improperly and for too long on the computer. I can sense the pain. Then, occasionally at night, I experience aches in my fingers, as if I am having problems flexing them. The ache might then go away if I don't think about it too much.

After that, there are those fuzzy times when I can't remember where I put anything. When I look in the mirror, I see cottage cheese thighs and arms. I had my shorts on the other day and I caught a glimpse of my thighs and thought, *Oh no, cellulite!*

Up to this point, I never had any, and now it was there. I have seen cellulite before at the beach and a lot of it. I read an article to learn how to either help it or get rid of it. It is what it is to be honest. I also notice I have bingo wings. When I wave, they wave back, and there are dimples.

I started strength training, but after a week I didn't lift another weight. I wish I could be more dedicated to and dependable with my exercise routine. I am aware of what I must do, but sometimes it just requires action. Now that I know strength training, a healthy diet, and exercise are the key, it's sometimes difficult for me to put it into practice. I aspire to become more disciplined in the future. Then there is my turkey neck; I have looked for good creams for that and perhaps one day I will discover one.

I used to not give my neck much thought, but now I notice it whenever I look in the mirror. Perhaps I should just accept that I'm ageing. I'm getting older, and maintaining one's beauty and physical fitness requires a lot of work. At this point, I mean, it's not like I'm trying to fit in with anything or fit the beauty mold.

July 20, 2020

My colonoscopy was over ten days ago. I've had a lot of gas lately and feel bloated. I know they said I may experience this later, but I didn't think ten days later. I should probably be paying more attention to what I eat. "You are what you eat," they say.

I understand that eating carelessly has consequences. Only another glance at my muffin top reveals the extent of the damage, the hips do not lie either. It's all part of the middle-age spread. I've decided to keep a food diary of what I eat this week. Simultaneously, I intend to be more conscious of what I put into my body. I dislike feeling bloated.

It's amusing to talk about getting older with friends. It's an ongoing conversation, and we laugh about it all the time. We wonder where all those years went and how we got to this age so quickly. When I talk to people now, it's difficult to comprehend because it seems like only yesterday that we were joking around and doing silly things.

Then time flew by, and now we're in 2020. I've known one of my girlfriends since I was three years old. We used to talk about 2030 and how I'd be this age by then. It feels like that conversation was only a few days ago. Time seems to move slowly at first, then quickly. I'd never given it much thought until now.

Suddenly, I am of a certain age, and I witness discrimination. I used to laugh at it, but it's true. There is age discrimination everywhere. Sometimes it may be a job description and you have to be within a certain age category. To be honest, you are as young as you feel, and it all comes down to your attitude. "Age is nothing more than a number." It is about how you embrace it.

July 28, 2020

It's been four months and I haven't had a menstrual flow. Yes, that is cause for celebration once more, but anything is possible at this point. I need to go for the entire twelve months. The cycle will then come to an end, and I will enter menopause. That must be thrilling. I haven't experienced a hot flash for a while. It's been wonderful not having to deal with those.

During this time, I am content and haven't given them much thought. I've also tried to limit my caffeine consumption to two cups per day. I'm aware that I should try to eliminate coffee, but I enjoy that morning cup.

August 7, 2020

As the pandemic spreads around the world, Toronto remains in stage two. Because they are all concerned about bars reopening, health professionals want to see a steady decline in numbers. While some people are changing their behaviors to comply with COVID, others appear not to care. There are parties going on; there is no social distancing or mask wearing. Some people act as if nothing is happening.

Nonetheless, we are still amid a pandemic. There is much speculation about a second wave arriving in the fall. My girlfriend is in Australia, and they are currently experiencing a wave in some areas. Despite this, Australia has a relatively lower population density than some countries. My friend is a nurse, and she says they never wore protective gear during the pandemic until now. Prior to admission, everyone is tested.

I still feel like I'm in a time warp. People are going about their business as the economy is picking up five months later. The time is still surreal. Masks are essential, so I keep one in my bag whenever I go shopping. I'm not wearing a mask when I walk, but I am following my distancing rules and moving out of the way for people.

It still gets too much at times, but for now, I'm dealing with it. I'm exhausted just thinking about having to travel during this pandemic. I don't think I could sit on a plane for ten hours while wearing a mask. That would be excessive. When I put it on now, after a few minutes, I feel as if I need air. It is difficult to wear, but it must be done. Masks have suddenly become the fashion accessory of the new century. Who knows how long we'll need to wear them?

There are now 18 million cases worldwide, with over 700,000 deaths. I've never experienced or witnessed anything like this in my life. I had only heard of the plague and the Spanish flu. Everything is still fresh in the news, just as it was in March. Every day, I learn about new cases. Some areas are doing better than others, but the problem remains. The whole world is experiencing the pandemic.

In Canada, they are discussing pandemic measures, such as mask wearing and physical distancing, for the time being. When I go out, I am even more skeptical. Going out is becoming, and continues to be, a chore. I need to make certain that I have all the pandemic necessities in my bag, including the mask. This is required, and without it, some establishments may refuse entry.

We are still enjoying pleasant weather in Toronto, which is a plus. Being able to get out and get some fresh air has been a lifesaver.

Meanwhile, my hot flashes and night sweats have returned. Last night was a disaster. I was sweating profusely and had to use the restroom several times. I awoke this morning with a severe migraine. I haven't had one in a long time. I'm not feeling well today.

The symptoms have returned, but not having them was enjoyable while it lasted. I've just been trying to get through each day since the pandemic. There are times when I can't get out of bed. It's not easy mentally, and I know I'm not the only one who is struggling.

After talking with others, it seems we all feel the same way. While I try to keep myself busy, it can be difficult at times. I still appear to be struggling since I reached fifty. I know I'm supposed to be more experienced, but the changes I'm experiencing, as well as the women's issues, can be difficult at times. Without a doubt, I am grateful to have reached this age. I am fortunate. I am aware that some people do not reach this age. To be honest, it is challenging; well, for me it is.

August 14, 2020

The pandemic continues, and as the world relaxes restrictions, the virus spreads. The numbers and cases continue to rise. There is currently no vaccine, and we are most likely looking at 2021, but even then, it will not be immediate. Governments are scrambling, and everyone is talking about children returning to school in September, including here in Toronto.

I've been trapped in my own bubble for the past five months, and it's been difficult. However, I am aware that I must simply keep going, even if it is not always easy. My hot flashes have reappeared, and I'm not sure how long they'll last. I must remind myself that these are not permanent circumstances. If I am not thinking about or experiencing them, I'm simply happy.

It's not just my perimenopausal symptoms, though; I'm still struggling with my diet. I still feel bloated at times. I woke up the other day at 55.8kg and felt depressed. I weighed myself today and came in at 55.2, so I'm feeling a little better. Why is food such a challenge now that I'm fifty?

The number on the scale will show me when I've overindulged. I do try to eat healthily overall. After discovering my husband was diabetic during a trip to Italy in 2016, we gradually changed our eating habits. It's difficult to imagine our frequent trips to Italy and how much food we'd consume. It was all about the food, in fact, throughout our three-week vacations, we would eat and eat and eat.

The invitations began to arrive once the town learned we had arrived. It can, however, become overwhelming at times. Growing up in England, I would only eat one meal at a time. Not three or more courses of good food in one sitting. Italians eat bread with every meal, and bread was something my husband really enjoyed. He has reduced his consumption of bread as part of our dietary change. We've mostly changed our diet now, and he's lost some weight.

It's funny because in Italy, we ate a lot of pasta and always enjoyed the dishes made by our family and in the restaurants. Pasta is no longer our preferred dish. We probably eat it once a week. Sometimes we don't even have a plate of pasta in a week.

(HOT FLASH) It's arrived, and I'm feeling hot in my face, neck, and body. I am just having a moment, but this is what it is like. There are also other symptoms, such as brain fog and moments when I get forgetful. They appear to be happening.

I feel like I'll be debating and fighting with food for the rest of my life. I am aware that I am fortunate and grateful for food. Even when conversing with girlfriends over time, food, diets, appearance, and looks have always been hot topics of discussion. "I'm going to start my diet and do better on Monday." Why Monday after a week of bingeing?

Then we talk about weight, thunder thighs, cellulite, and bat wings. I see these changes, but I am not concerned. Maintaining a commitment to exercise, on the other hand, can be challenging. But, thanks to YouTube, I've discovered some fabulous fifty gurus. I'll exercise whenever I feel like it. My issue is that I am not consistent.

There are days when I just can't be bothered. And then there's my hair. It is now turning white, not all over. I never colored my hair until I was forty. Now I do, and I will do so until I am ready to embrace my white hair. As a temporary measure, I also purchased an over-the-counter color stick.

Why are we women always so hard on ourselves?

August 19, 2020

For the past week or so, it appears that when I wake up in the morning, I am drenched and completely flashed out. For a while, I seemed to be cruising through my days with no hot flashes. I enjoyed those days and forgot about everything else, even though it was only temporary. You should always appreciate the times when your perimenopausal symptoms are under control. I was hoping that was the end of it.

As I am approaching my fifth month without a period, it's nice not to have to deal with my monthly menstrual at this point. I'd say it all started in February to March of last year, when I started to notice my monthlies were changing. I had one for a few days, then it got longer. Sometimes it was light brown, and as the months passed, I wondered what was going on.

My episode on the cruise felt like I had my period for a week in nine hours. I noticed changes over the next few months. Lighter monthly, no monthly, and seeing brown stuff until February 2020. I haven't had a period since March 2020, and August 2020 is my fifth month without one. I'm hoping I don't have a relapse and can keep going until March 2021, when I'll officially enter menopause soon after.

The thing is, it appears to be a long way off, and with the way my body is changing, you never know. Every month without one is a watershed moment. This transition period will require patience and time.

I'm still trying to make sense of this pandemic. As the month of August progresses, much of the talk now revolves around the children returning to school in September. Even though, children in some countries are already in school. We'll just have to wait and see what happens. On my walk today, I went through the park and saw parents and heard all these high-pitched voices talking.

For a moment, everything appeared normal. I've walked through the park before and saw nothing, only yellow tape, and a deserted play area. Strangely sad and empty. It was nice to hear children laughing and climbing, swinging, and generally having a good time. The truth is that it is far from normal. I'm still not comfortable being out in public. I have my small circle of friends, but I'm not going out just to be out. My perspective has shifted since March.

I texted my girlfriend the other day, and she told me she was feeling down and finding it difficult to get motivated. I told her I understood; I, too, have days when I struggle to get motivated. I can't always be cheerful, no matter how hard I try. Living through this pandemic is obviously having some effect on our mental health.

September 1, 2020. My dear friend Georgianna has left us.

September 13, 2020

Today, I'm still exhausted and covid fatigued. The last two weeks have not been pleasant. On September 1, my dear friend lost her battle with blood cancer. She fought valiantly until the bitter end. I knew she was sick, but it all happened so quickly in the end. I'm sad and have a lot of mixed feelings about everything.

In Greece, I met my dear friend Georgianna, and our friendship lasted twenty-six years. We were both the same age and were born on the same day. We would have celebrated our 51st birthday in a few weeks. It is still unreal. I'm currently lost in my own thoughts. Even during difficult times, she was a fighter who never stopped smiling. I'll miss her terribly.

I last saw her in August 2018, shortly after she was diagnosed, and I am grateful that I did. It would be the last time we laughed and talked about the good old days. We stayed in touch through technology, but it's not the same as being there in person.

I still can't believe I'll never talk to my dear friend again. I am relieved that she will no longer be in pain at this point. I'll remember her smiling face and the wonderful memories and times we had in Greece. My trips to the village where she lived and worked hard, milking goats, tending to bees, picking olives, or preparing pistachio nuts.

Georgianna did everything. She was a great comedian, always with a big smile on her face. Not to mention the best Greek cook ever, she made the most delicious homemade Greek food I'd ever had. (Gemista) stuffed peppers with rice, was one of my favorites, as was fasolada, Greek beans done in the pressure cooker. They were great times, and I will cherish those memories for the rest of my life.

I was in Quebec for a few days, only to realize I wouldn't be home for my dear friend's farewell. I zoomed in to be a part of the moment and chat session as a symbol of our current times. This was something I had to do while driving back home to Toronto. We would often talk and laugh about all the fun things that came with ageing as we both aged at the same time. We had so much fun, and I will be eternally grateful for having such a wonderful friend. She was a good one who left us far too soon. May she rest in peace.

Since I turned fifty, all I seem to hear about are health-related issues, problems, and deaths. Is this how it will be from here? It appears to be all so dismal. But there will be light along the way, I am confident.

It will be six months since my last menstrual cycle. Although I don't miss it, I still must deal with all the perimenopausal issues. I'm hoping it all gets better. I still crave a good night's sleep these days; I'm lucky if I get three or four uninterrupted hours of sleep in a row. Things can only get better from here. I certainly hope so. Maybe it'll improve once I stop thinking about it all the time. It's difficult not to let it all get to you.

It's My Birthday!

September 25, 2020

On this day, fifty-one years ago, I was born. I have the impression that I am old. Aging can be a strange thing at times. On some days, I feel like a spring chicken, and on others, I feel my age. I feel blessed and fortunate to have reached another birthday.

At the same time, I'm sad today. My friend, who died on September 1, would have celebrated today with me. We would wish each other well today and for future birthdays. We often laughed about our past and our future, aches and all. It's still a little surreal. She is not here to share that moment with any longer.

My perimenopausal symptoms have returned in full swing. They fluctuate like my hormones. They're all over for some reason. My breasts felt heavy, in the last few days. I'm not sure what to think about that. I remember feeling like that when I was about to have my monthly period. But I'm about to enter my seventh month without one.

Nowadays, I have no idea how my body is feeling. There are days when I feel so drained and have little energy. It could also be the change in weather as we transition into fall. I dislike this stage of life and its constant changes. Not to mention that we have entered the second wave of this pandemic. It appears to be ongoing. It's like watching a never-ending story. It's strange and uncertain, and it's mentally taxing for everyone. It's all too much for me to bear. I know I am not alone; the entire world is living a nightmare.

Fortunately, we had some wonderful weather this summer, and the fall has been pleasant so far. Who knows what we can expect in the coming months as we approach flu season and cold season? Another shutdown is possible, but only time and human behavior will tell.

The COVID figures are mind-boggling. Almost one million people have died worldwide. I'm still dazed about it all. The new norm is to spend more time at home. It's as if I'm living on another planet right now. There is no end in sight, nor is there any good news on the vaccine front. Various countries are still researching and working to obtain one. I'm fine today, but the mental strain is too much for me at times. I've never witnessed anything like it in my life.

Sometimes, I try to move on and forget about it. When everyone is wearing masks, how can it be forgotten? It's like a nightmare; we have no idea when it will end. I'm hoping it's sooner rather than later.

It's a beautiful day outside today. We've had some beautiful weather, but it's likely to cool down as fall approaches. We are now being urged to get the flu shot this year. I've never gotten a flu shot before and have no plans to start now. I'll just have to stock up on vitamins and other essentials.

Hopefully, I'll be able to avoid getting sick. I will continue to wear my mask, wash my hands, sanitize them, and adhere to the behavioral guidelines. We can overcome this if we all do our part.

October 2, 2020

The leaves are changing and falling off the trees. It's beginning to look a lot like fall. This is my favorite time of the year. It's so lovely, and I always appreciate the colors, leaves, drives, and other seasonal elements. I've decided to continue ignoring what's going on around me.

After seven months, it continues to be exhausting. The main story this morning is that the U.S. president and his wife both tested positive for COVID. This is the breaking news of the moment. As the world grapples with it all, I, for one, need a break. I have my own women's issues to deal with, such as my changing body, hormones, hot flashes, and mood swings, which continue.

With the arrival of cooler weather comes a loss of motivation. Who wants to go out in the cold in Canadian winter if they don't have to? Oh well, I'll have to resume my YouTube workouts at home. I just need to get motivated.

As I enter the seventh month, I still haven't had a period. I'm still having hot flashes. You never know when it'll appear, you just suddenly feel its presence. When I'm not experiencing one, I'm always happy. But one never knows. If I'm having a good day, I just enjoy it and am grateful. This week I haven't been sweating profusely in bed. It hasn't been all that bad. I'm feeling fine, but anything can happen.

I'm still having trouble sleeping, and this has been going on for nearly a year. I'd be content just to get a few hours of uninterrupted sleep. That isn't usually the case with my frequent midnight or early morning bathroom visits. I've even tried not drinking for several hours before going to bed. Nothing seems to work; I always wake up in the middle of the night.

October 16, 2020

What a night. Three-bathroom visits, tossing and turning, unable to sleep again. Ahhh, I'm hot and sweaty. I awoke this morning exhausted. There is no other way to put it. That is exactly how I feel. I just wish I could go back to my adolescence. Those days when I could sleep for ten hours or more and feel like I got a good night's sleep. I need to change something; I feel as if I've been saying it forever, like a broken record. I need to concentrate and try to make a change.

The hot flashes have been manageable this week. It's such a relief when a week passes, and they haven't been going all out. All of this, however, can change from day to day. I'm still fighting a losing battle with my diet and what I eat.

Last week was not a good one. I ate like a pig and suffered the consequences. Weight is an ongoing topic for women, and while it should not define you, it does. I was walking outside the other day when I noticed my reflection in the window. Oh, wow. I thought my stomach appeared large, and I didn't like how it looked. I felt I had to do better. It didn't help that it was only a few days after Thanksgiving.

On Thanksgiving, you eat a meal that includes pumpkin pie. It's fantastic with cream. Naturally, I had to eat a piece or two or three until it was gone. I mean, I don't overindulge all the time. Sometimes I wonder, "Why not?" I should be gentler with myself. Why can't I have a pumpkin pie or a piece of chocolate every now and then? Eight months into a pandemic and uncertain times, why shouldn't I indulge?

As the pandemic progresses and cases increase, new rules have emerged. Some people continue to refuse to follow the rules. Certain areas in Toronto and the surrounding GTA have gone back in time to help slow the spread. There are no indoor dining options. Gyms have been closed for the second time for twenty-eight days.

Unfortunately, people are still dying. The same thing is still happening on a global scale. Many people still work from home. People are still losing their jobs, and large corporations are continuing to reduce their workforce. Industries are not rebounding quickly. Thousands are now looking for a small piece of the global job market. These are trying times.

One good thing is that the weather in Canada is still relatively mild. The sun is shining today, and I can go for a walk. I'll be content if I can accomplish this. Walking and listening to music has helped me cope with the pandemic. It's my form of escape and will remain so. I always keep my physical distance in mind. I dread the real winter months when it snows and you can't even go outside because it's too cold.

October 22, 2020

The covers were on and off last night. My legs were restless as per usual. I went to the bathroom at midnight and again at 2 a.m. When morning came, I rolled out of bed exhausted. I couldn't help but cry. It's a shambles. All I want is a good night's sleep. Even four uninterrupted hours would be welcome at this point. Is that too much to hope for? What's the deal with all of this?

I'll have to go back to the internet and look up sleep aids. I did experiment with an over-the-counter herbal melatonin sleep aid. The issue is that it didn't work. I require assistance. This lack of sleep is driving me crazy. I haven't slept well in such a long time that it's difficult to believe. I just need some uninterrupted sleep. My body requires it, and it's tough.

Sleep is essential, even as you get older. I understand that, but my sleep issues persist, and I am always exhausted. I still haven't cut the caffeine; I know it's necessary, and I'll have to investigate alternative methods to help. It's really wearing on me; my eyes are dark and I'm not feeling well. I will enter my eighth month without a period in November and I have to say, not having to contend with this has been a relief. I just hope it lasts one whole year because then I'll be in menopause.

That's very exciting. Perhaps the best is yet to come. Nobody really prepared me for this. There isn't even much discussion about it with your doctor. People make fun of it, but it isn't a joke, and I believe we should have more information about what to expect and all the resources to be explored prior to it. What can we really expect during this extended period of our lives?

The changing body can be overwhelming at times. I'm dealing not only with perimenopause but also with a pandemic. Even though I try hard not to listen anymore, it still happens from time to time. The figures, the case counts, the deaths.

As we enter November, there is still no clear timeline for a vaccine. This could go on for a long time. We can only hope. I think the best way to deal with it is to zone out. As a distraction, I try to watch Italian television. I enjoy drama shows. They remove me from reality. I also listen to Greek music, which takes me back to my time in Greece and makes me think of my friend who recently passed away. I never really appreciated the music when I lived there, but now I love it.

For many years, Greece was the place where we would meet and share wonderful memories. Now, listening to Greek music is my way of escaping from what's going on. I'm trying hard to get on with it. Just like everyone else. It will all pass. Then we can look back and remember the strange times. We'll make it through.

November 3, 2020

For the past week, I've been limiting myself to one caffeinated beverage in the morning and turning off devices two hours before bedtime to listen to relaxing music and read. I require a miracle. It's insane; I never imagined that at this point in my life, sleep, mood, and all the other hormonal issues would have such an impact. As a rule, I dislike taking any kind of medication. If possible, I prefer to let things go.

As a result, I just keep going, even though my sleep is still not great. I simply accept it. If anything, I know that only I can make a difference. But seriously? Even melatonin isn't helping. What else can I do?

I'm still paying my regular visits to the bathroom. My sleep is still only for a few hours, and the tale of sleepless nights continues. The sad thing is that once I get back into bed after using the restroom, I close my eyes but still can't seem to fall back asleep. So, instead of sleeping, I just close my eyes and stay in bed.

I've been trying hard not to think about the ongoing pandemic. We've been at this for eight months and counting, and the world is still dealing with the second wave of lockdowns. Throughout it all, I will try to fill my time as best as I can, continuing to travel from my couch via my YouTube cruises and bake the occasional banana loaf or two. Wow, look at me!

November 5, 2020

It's 3 a.m., and I need to use the restroom. Previously, it was at 2 a.m. that I was automatically waking up. With the recent time change, I guess it's now 3 a.m. again. I rolled out of bed at 5:15 a.m., exhausted once more. When I looked in the mirror, my eyes were dark as they have been for a while now.

This is to be expected as each night passes and I am deprived of sleep. All I want is a good night's sleep. I guess that's something I can only fantasize about these days. I've reduced my caffeine consumption and I am hoping to eventually wean myself off it.

When I think about my sleeping patterns and how bad they are, I just want to cry. This is usually the time of year when I go to my doctor for a physical, but with the pandemic going on, it's all different. Maybe I should talk to my doctor about my sleep problems. For now, my repetitive issues continue.

November 9, 2020

Another exhausting night has passed, and I'm beginning to sound like a broken record. Every night, it's the same old story. When I wake up in the morning, I wonder how I even manage to get through each day. I guess I do. I've drastically reduced my caffeine consumption, and I try not to drink anything after 10 o'clock in the morning.

My body simply needs to adjust. I simply cannot sleep; sleep is currently my adversary. I can't sleep if I go to bed too early. My night usually begins with me falling asleep for an hour or two. Then it's a bathroom visit in the early hours. I can't sleep once I'm back in bed. I close my eyes, but I'm not sleeping. The next thing I know, it's morning and I haven't slept.

When I look in the mirror, my eye bags are getting worse. My eyes have dark circles around them. Even melatonin capsules are unable to help me sleep through the night. Everything stinks right now. I am tired of it all and dislike this period in my life.

This is my eighth month without a period. It's one less thing to worry about, which is a good thing. My husband keeps telling me that the lack of sleep is all in my head. When he hits the pillow, he's out for the count and sleeping like a baby. I'd be content if I could only sleep like he did. However, he is not dealing with my women's problems, so enough said. Things can only get better from here. Michaela, think positively.

November 21, 2020

It's official: we'll be entering another COVID-19 lockdown on Monday. As the second wave continues, many people are dying. The region of Toronto and Peel will revert to how it was in March. Services that are not necessary will have to close. Only takeout and delivery services are permitted. We are advised not to travel to other areas in Canada that may be in a different time zone than us. They want to keep the spread under control. Hopefully, people will not go insane again with their rampant product buying and hoarding.

Fortunately, I have a hair appointment scheduled for today, right before we lock down. Who knows how my hair will look when I come out of the lockdown. It may even last until the Christmas holidays. Who knows when salons will reopen after a twenty-eight-day closure? Oh well, I went months without seeing a hairdresser during the first wave, so we'll see if I make it after the second lockdown.

My hot flashes, this week, have been a little less intense. I feel on top of the world when I am not experiencing them. They can be unpredictable at times. I wish I could have these hot flash-free weeks on a regular basis. The problem is that there is no chance of getting what I want, nor do I have a choice. I'm just going through the motions.

My sleep has also been good this week. No, I'm not claiming that it's been fantastic. I've had four hours of uninterrupted sleep for the past two nights. It's great, and I'm feeling a little better. I'm still having trouble falling asleep, but I'll take it. My ideal goal would be to get six to eight hours of uninterrupted sleep. That may be pushing it. I know my sleep is still a work in progress, and it will be for as long as I am going through menopause.

I am still trying to focus more on what I eat and be more conscious. I have to say I am proud of myself because I have eliminated a lot of my sugar intake. I still have a way to go, but I will get there. I did, however, purchase a bag of chips and consume five mint chocolates. This is my weekly treat. I've been excellent all week.

Sometimes I think I'm being too hard on myself. I'm trying so hard these days, for the most part. I feel like I've spent my entire life questioning myself and feeling guilty or bad after indulging. Now I realize that, with moderate amounts and limitation, I can enjoy a little chocolate now and then. It all comes down to balance.

The hot flashes have been minimal for some time. They appear to be gradually returning now. I've made the most of the hot flash-free days. I've been tossing and turning all night. After one trip to the restroom, I couldn't sleep again until 4 a.m.

Of course, these topics of discussion have recently come up again with my girlfriend. She, like me, is sleep deprived. We are not on our own, as we move through the so-called change, this is a struggle for many middle-aged women. Some of the women I know, though, do not even have perimenopausal symptoms or lack of sleep. I'm envious of them.

As we enter the month of December, it will be my ninth month without a period, and I appreciate it. Tampons and pads are no longer required. It's all too thrilling. I need to go twelve months without a period before I enter menopause. I'm not quite certain whether I should sing about it for now.

Will all my symptoms vanish overnight? I'm not so sure. Only time will tell. According to what I've heard, the changes will continue. It's funny because I occasionally feel like I should have my period every month. Some symptoms exist, such as tender breasts and an occasional craving for sweets and food indulgences. There are so many changes that a woman's body goes through during this stage, and to be honest, I don't like it. I just can't seem to accept everything; it's upsetting at times and just brings me down.

December 1, 2020

I received an unexpected text message from my brother in the United Kingdom today. He informed me that my mother had been admitted to the hospital earlier in the week because her blood level was at 40% and her blood was thin. The doctor advised her to stay in the hospital until her blood levels were restored. She'd also need to have a body scan and be out of the hospital in a few days. He gave me a telephone number to call to reach the acute medical unit, where she was admitted.

That news caught me completely off guard. I was at a loss for words at this point. I feared the worst, as one would. With the current pandemic situation, I didn't want to travel unless necessary. It was too late to call the hospital today, so I decided to try again tomorrow due to the five-hour time difference. That night, I went to bed and all I could think about was my mother. This was not the kind of news I was expecting. I was worried about what was wrong with her now.

December 2, 2020

I didn't get much sleep last night. That's nothing new given my current situation. My night was consumed by concern for my mother and the sudden drop in her blood volume. I awoke early, thinking to myself, "I need to contact the hospital and find out what's going on."

When I tried to call the number, I was given, the phone line rang and rang. There was no response. I tried several times, but to no avail. After numerous attempts, I was extremely frustrated. I informed my brother, who advised me to keep trying. With the current COVID situation, things must have been hectic in the hospitals, and I'm guessing no one was answering the phones.

Later that afternoon, I spoke with my brother, who informed me that my mother would not have a scan. Instead, he stated that they would perform a biopsy to determine what was wrong. He said she'd be released from the hospital on Friday, and he'd know more about what was happening then.

December 3, 2020

When I wake up each morning, apart from being tired, I never know what to expect from day to day or week to week. I just go with the flow. I think I was overly excited about my two better nights of sleep. My midnight bathroom trips and restless legs have returned.

After my bathroom visits, I can never fall back to sleep. I've been researching essential oils. Maybe I'll give those a shot. My friends have told me that they use a black cohosh supplement and cannabis oil to help with hot flashes. Perhaps I should buy something to help me. Is there anything I can do right now to help my erratic sleeping habits? I'm so sick of it all, and my broken record continues playing.

As the pandemic continues, the current lockdown will be in place until December 21. We'll see what happens next. In our province of Ontario, there are a high number of cases, and all necessary stores are closed again. I'm still mentally drained from it all. I've drastically reduced my COVID-19 news consumption. It is the most effective way to deal with it all right now. Where has 2020 gone? It's as if I turned around and it was almost gone.

As the year ends, it has been one of the strangest, saddest, and craziest. There was so much hope for a new decade at the start of the year, but instead there is now so much pain and suffering all over the world. Yes, these are trying times for those of us struggling. There always appears to be something going on. It is easy to feel hopeless during these times.

I talked to my brother again today. He stated that my mother refused to have an MRI. My mother is on heart medication after suffering a mild heart attack several years ago. He stated that they performed the biopsy and that stem cells were extracted from her. He stated that they might let her out tomorrow, but they wanted to see if her blood levels had improved first.

Once we get the results, we will see what is going on. I tried again to call her at the hospital, and this time, the first thing I was greeted with was a message about COVID and how no visitors were allowed in the hospital. Trying to get through was a nightmare, especially calling internationally.

After numerous attempts, I finally got through. I was able to speak with my mother; she sounded OK, she just needed to rest. Now we need to wait and see the results, which could take up to two weeks. Hopefully then, we would know the real prognosis.

December 4, 2020

It is 3:38 a.m., I am wide awake, tossing and turning. My body is warm, and I'm having hot flashes. I'm not sweating as much as usual, but I need to get out of bed. At 4:32 a.m. I stand up and examine myself in the mirror. My eyes are horrifying. I look exactly how I feel: wrecked and worn-out.

Everything is too much. My thoughts are also elsewhere, as I consider my mother, who is in the hospital during these trying times. It's not just one relative I'm thinking about; my aunt is currently battling cancer and has been in and out of hospitals fighting infections. Even though my situation is not as dire as theirs, it is taking its toll mentally.

My mother was released from the hospital. She couldn't wait to leave. She dislikes being out of her own comfort zone. At the very least, she was back home, which was a relief. It was a stressful moment for all of us, worrying and questioning what was wrong with her.

December 7, 2020

My mother appeared to be in decent health, or I thought she was, until I received that text from my brother. I know she takes medication for her heart, as well as pills for her rheumatoid arthritis in her hands. She had suffered for years with her hands, which had become slightly deformed; she was unable to open jars or other items because she had lost her grip.

Another issue for her was that her vision had slowly deteriorated. She had gone in to have surgery on one of her eyes for cataracts and came out with blurred vision. The procedure took several hours before she came out, and when she did, her eye was not right. The next thing I knew, she had to wait over a year for it to be fixed because they kept postponing her appointments. It didn't help that it happened during the COVID pandemic. In the meantime, she was given European lenses to see if they could help. Her eyes were never the same after that.

I frequently called my mother to check in on her and see how she was doing. She stated that she was doing well after being in the hospital. Her motto was, "No matter what, just get on with it," and she did just that.

December 16, 2020

This week has been all about vaccines. The first recipient in the United Kingdom was a ninety-year-old woman, and other countries are now in the process of rolling it out. I'm sick of hearing about COVID. I have other concerns right now, and having a vaccine is not one of them. Aside from the vaccine discussion, my thoughts and concerns about my mother remain.

We've talked a few times, and she appears to be fine right now. Hopefully, we will know what is happening soon. Why is it that when you're waiting for something, it can seem like an eternity? Later that evening, I learned my mother has acute myeloid leukemia, with a bleak prognosis.

December 17, 2020

My early morning sweats continue. My clothes are wet, and I frequently feel like my heart is pounding rapidly. I'm completely drained. The previous week was similar. The bad news from back home yesterday didn't help matters.

2020 could not have been a more disastrous year. The year 2021 might not be much better. I'm trying to get a full picture. My mother has stated that she does not want chemotherapy and prefers blood transfusions. My family is texting me to tell me all the news.

I rely on them to keep me informed of what is going on. I spoke with my relatives and asked them to be supportive and positive for mum during this difficult time. It's difficult to hear this news while living in another country. Even I am not feeling particularly upbeat these days, what with my own womanly woes and all this COVID nonsense. It can be stressful at times. Although it pales in comparison to learning about my mother's illness.

I don't usually spend Christmas in England, and during a pandemic, I'm not sure whether I should go. On the other hand, I do not want to sit around, though. At this point, however, I do not know the true prognosis, which we will learn soon. Even though we have received this terrible news, my mother's attitude remains the same: "You just have to get on with it." I completely agree.

However, I am not dealing with such a diagnosis like she is. She does have her entire family nearby, and if anything, I would be there in a heartbeat. I am not a fan of technology, but currently, it is convenient to be able to FaceTime and video chat with those closest to me.

I tried to reach her doctor to find out what was wrong. The issue is that when you are not in the same time zone, it can be difficult to find the right moment. I'm just curious about the prognosis and how everything looks. She was in the hospital receiving blood on Tuesday, and it appears that this will become a weekly occurrence. She was pale when I spoke to her, but knowing my mother, she will keep going. Meanwhile, my cancer-stricken aunt recently contracted COVID-19 and has been hospitalized several times.

I can't wait for this year to be over. Given the current situation in Toronto, I believe the lockdown will be extended. That is fine with me. Everyone should have been put on lockdown for a while. Even though Toronto is closed, I can drive up north and shop. It simply doesn't make sense. We've been in this pandemic for almost a year.

Despite my best efforts to avoid anything related to COVID-19, it's in your face no matter which way you turn. Brutal reminders of how we're still in the thick of it. It hardly looks like Christmas. Apart from the pretty lit-up houses and a dusting of snow. This year will undoubtedly be different.

I cannot imagine how children are dealing with this whole pandemic. Such strange times and it continues.

December 23, 2020

What an eventful week. My usual symptoms persist, and I am now experiencing night sweats around 4 a.m. These symptoms typically change from week to week. I'm not so bad during the day.

Meanwhile, our lockdown in Toronto has been extended due to an increase in the number of cases.

Lockdowns look the same all over the world, but these holidays are unique. I don't even want to celebrate. After all, what is there to celebrate as 2020 ends? According to reports, there are 78 million cases and 1.7 million deaths worldwide.

We'll have to wait and see what happens next. On the plus side, vaccines have been distributed in recent weeks. Healthcare workers, frontline workers, and the elderly and vulnerable populations will be given preference. It may not be available until late next year to all those who want to take it. Although I haven't given it much thought, this week's news story was, at the very least, the vaccine euphoria.

After just learning of my mother's blood cancer diagnosis, it isn't a good time for me right now. I'm still trying to recover from the shock. It's just another shocking piece of information. To hear it so close to the end of the year. I'm trying hard to be strong and keep it together. What makes it more difficult is that she is in the United Kingdom, and I am in Canada.

Under normal circumstances, I could have simply hopped on a plane and flown there to help. Not during COVID-19, when the dynamic appears to be different. I am currently unable to do so.

Fortunately, she has her family to lean on, so she is not alone. Although she is not technologically savvy, FaceTime will become a routine part of our communication so that I can see her. It's very frustrating, but this is how it will be for the time being. This is one of the realities that no one wants to face when they choose to live apart from their family.

I attempted again to contact her doctor but was unsuccessful. Being only a few days away from the holidays does not help. So far, all I know is that she must have a blood test one day and a transfusion the next. This will occur every week. My mind and thoughts are in the United Kingdom today, as they have been since hearing the news. She will receive a blood transfusion today, which could take up to six hours. At this point, I don't even know what the prognosis is, which makes things even more difficult.

Mom has chosen not to have chemo, as it would have been ineffective given her age and health complications. We must honor her wishes. Right now, everything is a mess. A virus variant that is causing concern is apparently circulating in the U.K. It's like an endless loop of constant COVID-related news. Travel to England would be difficult right now.

To put it mildly, these are difficult times. Christmas and the holidays will be a little quieter around the world, as everyone struggles to cope with the pandemic. Due to restrictions on non-essential travel, it may not be as busy. What perplexes me is how often people are still willing to travel during these times.

I couldn't bear the thought of sitting on a plane for hours with a mask on, unsure of who is infected with the virus. I don't need to travel right now. If something happens at this point, I may not have a choice, but for the time being, safety comes first. Also, because my mother is ill, I don't want to take any chances and risk bringing an infection into her home.

Merry Christmas!

December 25, 2020

Merry Christmas, and what a strange one it is this year. It only seems like yesterday that I was sitting with people, laughing and in close quarters, with not a care in the world. Things will be drastically different in 2020. It is just my husband and me. We didn't eat as much this year and we drank very little. I only had a quarter glass of wine with dinner. I was simply not in the mood.

We did FaceTime with my family, and it was difficult to watch and talk to my mother. She appears pale and frail now. This is when I appreciate technology the most. Her entire family was present, which is critical in these current circumstances. The diagnosis is still difficult to comprehend because it came from nowhere.

At this point, I am still stunned. I'll have to wait until December 30. I should then be able to communicate with the hematology nurse who is caring for her. I'm hoping for a clearer picture and an update on the situation.

As we begin the new year, I have just completed my ninth month without my monthly period. January will mark the tenth month. I'm sure the hot flashes and aches and pains will persist. The same record keeps playing continuously. It's just my constant reality.

December 28, 2020

We got through Christmas and Boxing Day and without the excess food. In previous years, we usually ate a lot more and felt bloated by the end of the day. A January 1 diet would then be at the top of my priority list for the new year. It is when gyms start promoting memberships and getting you in the best shape of your life. The problem is that we want to believe it all, only to find out that it's all over in a month and we're back to square one.

There is far too much emphasis on our weight, what we should look like, and comparing ourselves to our everyday influencers. This year, I must say because I never overate, I feel fine. It's all about having the upper hand. Previously, at Christmas, some of the eating was mindless and solely for the occasion. I think buying a lot of candy and unnecessary items is a force of habit, but now that I'm older, I don't feel the need to eat poorly all the time. I still enjoy treats, but not to the same extent that I used to.

Finally, I feel more in control, which is a victory for me. What will my 2021 resolution be now that I don't have to worry about my weight in the new year?

But first and foremost, I wish my mother a speedy recovery and good health. Another wish would be to get rid of COVID-19 and go back to normal. Finally, get rid of my hot flashes and let me sleep like a baby. One can always wish for things, but they may not always come true.

Let there be hope, then perhaps my night sweats, sleep problems, and hormonal changes will go away, and I won't see or hear about them again. If only my sweats would stop appearing around 3 to 4 in the morning, that would be great. They chop and change all the time, just like the weather.

So far, I have yet to purchase the recommended supplement that is supposed to alleviate hot flashes. Black cohosh is the name, and some people I've talked to say it helps to tone down the flashes. My problem is that I can be a procrastinator at times. You'd think I'd have gotten around to buying some and at least trying it by now. Maybe before the end of the year. In the meantime, I'll just have to suffer.

December 30, 2020

I spoke with my mother's hematologist today, and the news was worse than I had anticipated. My mother may not have long to live; it hit me like a punch in the stomach during our conversation. I'm sad and gutted because, just when I thought things couldn't get any worse, they did. All I want is to be able to fly home and hug my mother. The problem is that I can't right now, and I'm feeling helpless. The nurse was extremely helpful and comforting.

Following that conversation, I'll need to make a conference call to the United Kingdom to discuss the next steps and my mother's care. Her illness is incurable, and she will deteriorate over time. But how long does she have? I'm not sure. I am heartbroken beyond words. I chose to leave my home country many years ago.

At times like this, I wish I was closer and not trapped by a spreading pandemic. I'm just taking each day and night as it comes right now. When the phone rings, I fear the worst. I'm tired now; Tomorrow, I must wake up early for this conference call with her doctor and the nurse, who are caring for her. I need to sleep because I'm exhausted and terrified of this new reality.

You usually hear about other people going through difficult situations. This is our family now, and it hurts. We're all still stunned. Everything is moving so quickly. I need to lower my head and go to sleep right now.

December 31, 2020

I awoke at 3 a.m. last night and didn't sleep a wink. My thoughts are still with my mother in England. I tossed and turned for an hour before finally getting up at 4:50 a.m. in the morning. The phone rang, and I was already on the line. The doctor and nurse were present, as well as my brother and mother, who were both quiet.

The doctor started the conversation and informed us that her type of cancer is a rapidly progressive and incurable disease. Acute myeloid leukemia. The only thing that can be done for her right now is to provide supportive care.

When it came to the subject of prognosis, my mother left the room and gave permission for it to be discussed with my brother and me. I had to bite my lower lip as they explained what was going on with her white cells, which were not looking good.

Still, I was just trying to process everything that had happened so quickly. Apparently, there was no detection of this until she did the bone marrow biopsy. The doctor mentioned that she had been asking my mother to do one, but she refused. It was not discovered until her blood count dropped and she was admitted.

According to what I was hearing, she could only have a few weeks or even a month to live. My mother is now adamant that she does not want help from caregivers. My brother currently lives with her and is available to help her.

The doctor mentioned that there may come a time when she does not want blood transfusions and that she must exercise caution.

I wish I could scream and cry right now. Flights from the United Kingdom have been canceled and only necessary travel is advised. My entire world has just crumbled. Tonight, will be spent at home in peace and quiet. I stayed in bed for part of the day. I'm numb and don't want to think about 2021. It stinks.

January 1, 2021

Best wishes for a prosperous New Year! I have no idea what will happen to me. Even though the year 2020 has come to an end, it has ended on a sad note for me because of my mother's diagnosis. For now, all I can do is take each day as it comes, check in with my mother via FaceTime whenever possible, and hope for the best. Her nurse stated that mom only needed support at this time, and fortunately, her entire family was there to support her. Acute myeloid leukemia is a particularly lethal form of leukemia.

I spoke with my brother and mother today; she is still pale. During the conversation, I was still struggling to digest the news from the last two weeks. There was no way of knowing how much time she had left on this planet. It could be a week, two weeks, a month, or two months.

Simply put, there was no set schedule. I'd have to brace myself for the worst and accept the possibility of being forced to return home in an emergency. She is not, at the very least, alone. If anything were to happen, my brother would contact me right away.

During my conversation with the hematologist and nurse, they mentioned that they would do whatever it took for me to travel at this time. They would give me a doctor's letter stating that my mother was nearing the end of her life and that I should be allowed to travel. It was hard to believe that things had gotten this drastic so quickly.

I requested a letter and a few days later, I received the letter via email. At least, should there be any emergency and a need to travel, I could get into the U.K. At this point, covid rules were changing by the minute. For some countries, you needed a travel covid test prior to your departure. At least 48 hours prior. Meanwhile, in Canada, the emphasis was on not traveling if you did not have to. Everything seemed so chaotic. For me, if I did need to go, then I would do whatever I needed to do.

January 3, 2021

I called my mother and spoke with her today. Despite her best efforts, I could detect a level of weakness in her voice that I had not previously noticed. She assured me that she was fine, as she always does. I just felt so helpless at that point. I didn't feel good after the call ended. Even though only essential travel is permitted at this time, I began looking into flights. Despite the rules, people have continued to travel. My situation would be different; if I needed to travel, then I would travel.

January 8, 2021

I haven't been feeling well for the past week. I've been struggling since hearing all this news about what's going on in my homeland. Yes, I'm still trying to make sense of my mother's diagnosis. I've been struggling with it all, and given the circumstances, it's been nothing but stressful. When I'm sad, I sometimes feel like my head is going to explode.

Nonetheless, I know I must remain strong and travel to the United Kingdom as soon as possible. Right now, time is of the essence.

I'm an emotional wreck right now. I couldn't get out of bed yesterday; I just hid under the covers. I pottered around before returning to my bed again. My thoughts are making me feel down. I've had a few conversations with my mother, and she doesn't sound good. It's so difficult when I call her. I can feel her slipping away, and all I need to do is get there in time.

Everything happened so quickly that it's surreal. If there are no cancellations, I plan to leave early next week. The United Kingdom has recently implemented new rules requiring a negative COVID-19 test before boarding. I scheduled an appointment for tomorrow. It's not an easy moment for me.

I finally bought the black cohosh that everyone seems to swear by. I took it for four days, and my hot flashes seemed to get worse during that time. Because I am not the most patient person, I decided to discontinue use immediately. My sleep is still an issue, even though I purchased caffeine-free coffee. I'll continue to try to cut out real coffee from my diet.

Everything is a little much right now. I'm doing my best to keep it all together. I truly am. I'm just hoping my test results are negative. Vaccines are currently dominating the news. My mind is all over the place. Right now, all I can think about is getting there in time to see my mother. That's it.

January 9, 2021

I had to start looking at flights; though, getting a direct flight at this time of year to Manchester is not possible. My husband is unsure whether he should travel because he is diabetic, which is another health concern during these times. If he decides to come, he will also need to take a COVID test.

After some thought, he went to get his test and, like me, had to wait for the results. Later that day, my brother called me from the United Kingdom to tell me that my mother had been admitted to the hospital. Her throat was infected, and she was breathing irregularly. That did not sound promising. I told my brother I'd look for a flight and call him tomorrow to check in and see what was going on.

The search for a flight to Manchester, U.K, began. The problem was that there were no direct flights at this time of year. The path would always be via another gateway. Depending on the airline, most likely London. Flight prices appear to have risen unexpectedly during this pandemic, even though there are currently no restrictions on travel. I would not be considering travel if it were not for my current circumstances, especially not during these difficult times. However, this type of travel was necessary.

After several hours, we were able to secure overnight flights with Air Canada to London on January 11, to arrive early in the morning. We were able to obtain a compassionate fare because my mother was nearing the end of her life. We still had flights from London to Manchester to book. We found connecting flights to Manchester with British Airways, but the first flight was at 2:30 p.m. So, we reserved our seats.

In the past, I've been able to jump on an earlier flight without incurring any fees. The most important thing was that the flights have been scheduled, and I will be flying to see my mother. I'm just hoping that we make it in time. I'm still in shock. I thought she had more time than a week, maybe a month, not just a few days, as it is sounding.

January 10, 2021

Suddenly, I find myself booked on a flight to visit my mother. She might be dying, and it all happened out of nowhere. I'm thinking, *What if I bring COVID with me when I see her?* We're hoping they'll let us into the hospital. The entire scenario is a nightmare. We must pack, ensure that we have our COVID information, and download the government requirements for the U.K.

Later in the day, I'll call and speak with my brother. I have too many things to do right now, and my mind is racing. I want to sit down and cry. I'm clear I can't. I must keep going and do what needs to be done. My brother texted me to tell me that many members of my family have gathered at the hospital to support my mother. He stated that things are not looking good because she has pneumonia.

My brother called again about an hour later to say he had spoken with the hematologist and that my mother might only have a few hours or days to live. I couldn't believe what I was hearing. My first thought was that this had to be something serious that had been going on for a long time. It's all happening far too quickly.

My only conclusion at the time was that we needed to get there and see her before she passed away. We can only hope that we arrive on time. We are not looking forward to the flight and the prospect of wearing a mask for six to seven hours. I already get anxious when I fly and having to keep my mask on would be an added stress.

Still, I need to keep working on my preparations. Within a week, it appears she deteriorated rapidly. She had stopped eating and was no longer taking some of her medications. My brother also mentioned that the inside of her mouth was extremely sore.

The situation did not sound promising, and I needed to get started packing for the trip. I'd have to call my brother later that evening to find out how she was doing. We only needed to organize ourselves now, and we'd be ready to go. Fortunately, we had a flight leaving at 9 p.m., so we spent most of that day making sure we had everything we needed for the trip, including masks, gloves, face shields, and hand sanitizer.

I'm always nervous about flying and I usually experience claustrophobia and a sense of being squeezed in during a flight. It's usually fine when I arrive at the airport.

However, I prefer to be the last person on the plane. The door will then close, and we will depart. I don't like sitting for long periods of time while my panic sets in. I recognize it's all in my head, but I don't have a choice. The good news is that my husband will accompany me for emotional support on the journey.

January 11, 2021

The last few days have been a nightmare of trying to book flights to the United Kingdom and organize everything from COVID tests to downloading government apps and filling out forms. I have frequent hot flashes and tension headaches. I'm feeling tired right now. It's all too much to bear.

My mother's health is deteriorating rapidly. Our family members are all at her bedside, and now we're just hoping to get there in time to see her. It is a critical time, and she must be nearing the end of her life because the entire family was allowed to see her, even during COVID. My mother is currently in the hospital and appears to be fighting for her life. My only thought is, *I hope we get there in time*.

My brother told me yesterday that her hematologist had informed him that she only had a few hours or days to live. *Oh my god*, I thought, *what am I hearing?*

This whole situation has happened so fast. I am just still so shocked by everything. Later, after a conversation with my brother, he said he had taken more clean clothes to the hospital. He also mentioned they were trying to relieve the dryness in her mouth and that she was currently stable.

That was good to hear at the time because we had a flight booked. We only needed to get on that plane and hope we made it in time. Tonight, we'll board our flight to the United Kingdom. Time could not come quickly enough. I spent most of today in the bathroom with nerves in my stomach, not to mention the stress of it all. So many thoughts have raced through my mind. I'm not sure what to think.

January 12, 2021

My husband and I arrived at Heathrow airport at 8:30 a.m., after a six-and-a-half-hour flight from Toronto. We managed to land in another country during a pandemic, but we still had another flight to catch. It felt like we were in a movie on the plane. The cabin crew was outfitted with masks, gloves, and plastic shields, and except when eating or drinking, we wore masks the entire flight.

This is something I will remember for a long time. It was, however, not as bad as I had anticipated. I made it for the first leg of the journey, but there was still another flight to catch. Fortunately, the flight was relatively empty on the first leg. The problem was that we had to wait another six hours before flying from London to Manchester. This section of the flight is only forty minutes long. All I could think was, *Please do not pass yet, Mother, we are almost there.*

I'd flown on British Airways before, and from what I recall, I'd been allowed to board an earlier flight without being charged. I assumed we were early. Let's see if we could squeeze on an earlier flight.

I approached some ground agents and told them about my situation. The agent informed us that we would need to wait and made a phone call. She returned to me ten seconds later and said we needed to pay to change our flights. Meanwhile, there was no empathy or recognition. That was pretty much it. There was no attempt to help.

I moved to another desk and asked to speak with a manager. We were directed to another representative behind the desk. My simple request could not be fulfilled by the agent. Instead, he made excuses, claiming that our bags had been processed and that if we wanted to board the flight, we would have to wait. I simply wanted to speak with a manager. I was extremely dissatisfied with the situation. So, we waited nearly four hours to board our scheduled flight to Manchester.

We arrived at 4 o'clock in the afternoon and collected our luggage. The only thing on my mind was getting to the hospital in time to see my mother before she died. My nephew came to pick us up from the airport when we arrived in Manchester. We arrived at the hospital at 4:30 p.m. and went straight to her room.

We entered the room and went into the bathroom to wash our hands, still wearing our masks. There were some other family members present in her room. When I walked in, I noticed my mother was hooked up to oxygen and her eyes were closed. In such awful circumstances, I walked over to the side of the bed, hugged her, and began to cry. I believe she felt we had arrived. Her appearance was not good.

As I stared at her, she appeared frail, weak, and gaunt. She was using the oxygen mask to breathe. Then she started moaning and gasping. In my mind, I couldn't believe what was happening. We had made it, and she was aware of our presence. She wasn't saying anything, but she knew we'd arrived at the hospital.

Throughout her stay in the hospital, she'd had a steady stream of visitors. Due to the circumstances, many people have been permitted to visit her. She was in her own private room, due to her being near the end of life. My brother had been by her side the previous nights.

We were there now and would spend the night, sending him home to rest. I needed another cup of coffee around 10 o'clock to keep me awake. I was in the room with my mother, and I had made it, thank goodness. She had waited for us, and I was relieved that she was still alive when we arrived. The nurses had brought a bed into the room. My husband would simply sit beside her on that. When she was admitted, we knew she might only have a few hours or days to live.

At that point, everyone was just waiting for us to arrive. I was just glad to be there, holding her hand and wiping her sore mouth with water. I examined her frail hands, which were purple and bruised, most likely from blood transfusions. I had no idea a few months earlier that I'd be watching my mother slowly die from acute myeloid leukemia.

I am surprised as well as saddened by the drastic change in her appearance. She is now breathing, and the only thing we can do is continue to care for her as she approaches the end of her life. It's an extremely difficult situation, and I'm sick to my stomach as I observe it unfold. What really happened?

My husband encouraged me to come and rest. I'm afraid I can't. I can only watch my mother and be close by her side. It all appears to be a dream. But it's not a dream; it's real. She has been agitated all evening, and the nurses have entered the room to administer morphine and change her position. I'm just observing her groans; I don't want her to suffer any longer.

January 13, 2021

The night had passed, and it was 7 o'clock in the morning. The nurses arrived soon after with breakfast. They came into the room and asked if my mother needed anything, and I replied. I went out and ordered some toast and coffee. My mother's state had not changed at this point. When it got to 9 o'clock, some of my relatives arrived again at the hospital. My husband and I left to get showered and changed. Anything could've happened while we were gone.

When we returned, she was still breathing with oxygen. My mother appeared more relaxed than the night before. She seemed to be calm, but she was not present. My husband and I remained by her side. I could not take my eyes off her and stood the whole time at her bedside. I felt numb as I watched my mother near the end of her life. We spent the remainder of time with her.

As another evening began, my husband looked at me as we stood over her bed at 10 o'clock at night. He stated that he did not believe she would make it tonight. She was all set to go. He was correct; she died peacefully at 11:10 p.m. on January 13, 2021. We were present, but my mother had left. My husband walked over to the other side of the bed and informed me that she was gone.

Being in the moment was a surreal experience that I struggle with to this day. We notified the doctors, who arrived and examined her body.

Later, the chaplain entered and said a few words. My husband and I stayed in the room to spend this final moment with her in peace. She was gone. I was overcome with sadness as I stared at her lifeless body and her bruised hands from blood transfusions. This was my mother, the woman who brought me into the world and did an excellent job of teaching and instilling values in me.

It hurt that she was gone, so much. The numbness was intense; it was as if I were in a dream. I had a massive lump in my throat. I just stood dazed over her bed, irritated that I hadn't made it to the U.K. earlier during the pandemic. I was struggling and trying to reason with my own mind, so I never got to talk to her and tell her what was going on. At least, she was aware of our arrival in the room. She sensed we had made it from Canada. We were in that room, and she knew.

After a few hours, the hospital advised that they would come and remove her body and transport her to the morgue until funeral arrangements were made and the death was registered. I can't believe how quickly everything happened. She was admitted to the hospital on Saturday and was gone by Wednesday.

On Sunday, as she lay clinging to life, her room was packed with family members saying their final goodbyes. Fortunately, she seemed better on Monday. She is said to have stated that she would wait for us, and she did. My dear mother had died, and now, during a pandemic, arrangements would have to be made. We stayed with my mother for a few hours after she died.

I was at a loss for words, and all I wanted was to sit peacefully with her as she rested before they took her body away. I'd have to gather any of her belongings and transport them back to her house. It was a difficult moment. She was at peace now, and she would no longer need blood transfusions or deal with a painful mouth full of ulcers. She was no longer with us.

Everything happened far too quickly. Everything happened in an instant. It was far too quick. Why was it so quick? The only solace I have now is knowing that we were with her when she died, and she was not alone. She did not die of COVID, it was acute myeloid leukemia. I knew after a while in the room that we would have to leave and gather her last belongings.

We arrived at my mother's house around 2 a.m. We needed to get some rest. There was a void in her home. It's difficult to accept that she'll never walk through those doors again, and that we'll never hear her voice again. This is where I spent many years of my life before finding my own path.

The realization hit that this would be my final visit here, which is both difficult and sad to contemplate. The thought that she will never walk back through those doors breaks my heart and leaves me speechless. So many feelings: tears, sadness, and emptiness. Everything is so overwhelming. Norma Cummings was born on May 21, 1948; she died on January 13, 2021, she was 72 years old. I still can't believe it and I am lost beyond words.

January 14, 2021

We awoke, and I realized that things needed to be done and plans made. The next few days would be spent registering the death, calling the funeral home, and speaking with family members. It was a hectic time, trying to cancel her services and make funeral arrangements, despite her wishes to be cremated.

We had to figure out the service. It was not an easy time. I'd heard of leukemia but had no idea it came in different forms. My mother had aggressive acute myeloid leukemia. Given my mother's health issues, there was no treatment she could receive. My mother was adamantly opposed to all forms of chemotherapy.

I called the funeral home, and they said that once the death certificate was received, arrangements could be made. They also said that due to COVID, there was a thirty-person limit, and no flowers were allowed during these times. There may only be four people in the hearse and one photo on the coffin. We'd have to wait until January 28 to lay our beloved mother to rest. That would give us two weeks to collect our thoughts and make funeral arrangements. I am still in shock and disbelief.

January 15, 2021

The house was deserted; she was not present. The radio was dead; there was no life, no music from the 1960s. She enjoyed listening to the U.K Gold radio station and all the golden oldies. She was a huge admirer of the Kardashians. She thought they were all incredible and enjoyed the shows. She enjoyed coffee mornings and day trips with the women from her community center.

The sad thing was that because the United Kingdom, like much of the rest of the world, was in lockdown, not everyone could mourn or celebrate her life. Restrictions were imposed, and those who did not follow the rules faced fines. It was excruciatingly painful. These were not ordinary times or circumstances.

January 16, 2021

I'd spent the previous day or two trying to contact people to inform them of my mother's death. I went to the pharmacy to inform them about my mother's death and let them know they would no longer have to fill her prescriptions for her arthritis and heart medications. They were shocked to learn of her death. It was a stressful time registering her death and making funeral arrangements. There was no time to take a breather. The following week was spent making sure everything was in order.

After talking with other family members, everyone agreed that my mother had to have known she was sick for a long time. She, on the other hand, had not mentioned anything to anyone. This makes me both sad and angry. Who knows what she was thinking in those last moments? She even had three black masks in her kitchen drawer. One for my brother, who shared her home, one for myself, and one for my husband. These would be required for her funeral.

January 19, 2021

Her death had been registered, so we could now finalize the details and plans for the funeral. Her body would be taken to the chapel before cremation, and we would have one last chance to see it before the service. I needed to see my mother one more time. One last time, with a heavy heart, a sense of loss, and an empty feeling.

Following our conversation with the funeral director, he suggested we drop off some clothing for my mother. I can't believe I'm picking out clothes for my mother, who is no longer alive. Everything is a little overwhelming, and there is far too much going on. It all happened too quickly, and she was no longer present.

Over the next few days, we selected some clothes from her closet. We made sure she would look nice and chose an outfit she had never worn before. Once we had delivered the clothes, we would be able to see her body a few days later.

January 20, 2021

There was still work to be done, including sorting through her clothes and other belongings. Even though my brother would remain at home, as I was there, I needed to assist him with some of the tasks.

This way, he wouldn't have to worry about them later. I still had time to assist him before we left. The days were difficult, but we didn't have much time to sit because there was always something to be done or another relative to pay a visit to. During these terrible covid times, there were limits to people entering the home. It was such a sad affair.

My mother was the youngest of ten children, and two of her closest sisters lived nearby. I'd have to pay them a visit, even though we were supposedly under lockdown. One of the sisters was currently battling bowel cancer. I'd go up to my aunt's house and greet her at the door.

I couldn't hug, kiss, or make physical contact with my aunt and it broke my heart to see her so vulnerable at this time. She appeared weak and frail. Nothing like how she was a few years earlier; she was always upbeat and smiling. I loved my aunty, Carol. She hadn't seen my mother in a long time due to her own health problems.

I was aware that my wave might be the last time I saw her. It was the most difficult thing ever to see family and not be able to show any love or go inside their home under such terrible circumstances. These were extremely trying times.

January 24, 2021

Without my mother, there was silence throughout the home. She would frequently turn on the U.K Gold radio station when she got home, so I did the same. She was gone now, and she wasn't going to return. My mom was gone, and I still could not believe it; she was not going to stroll through that door, drop her bags, and say, "Put the kettle on."

I was still processing everything in my thoughts. Over and over in my mind, I keep thinking it happened so fast and then she was gone. There was not much time left, as January 28 would be my final goodbye. When we did view the body, it was not easy. I was able to bring some family photos and small objects to place in the coffin. She looked different, she was at peace, but it was hard. She looked lovely in the outfit we chose for her. I'm happy I had the opportunity to spend that time with her body.

January 25, 2021

I knew it would be challenging following my final encounter with my mother. I was aware that I would never be able to return to England in a hurry. I would not be seeing her again. This thought was a difficult concept to process. I used to return to England primarily because of my mother. Yes, I did see other individuals and relatives, but she was the reason, and she was gone now. I spent three weeks in

Manchester at the end of 2018 before departing for Italy, which was the last time I was in England.

During that time, I never thought a few years later, this would happen. Things happen in life, and life goes on.

January 28, 2021

On the day of the funeral, it was an ordinary gray day in Manchester. Some friends and relatives were gathered in front of my mother's house as it began to drizzle. Leaving her house for the final time, in the hearse, we would travel by the community center one final time and make our way to the crematorium.

There had been no time to contemplate until now. I spent all my time planning, determining who could go and who could not. There was a thirty-person maximum and that was it. If there was any overflow, they would have to wait outside. These were the strict COVID-19 rules in England at that time. Many of our relatives and some of her acquaintances were unable to attend.

Due to the U.K.'s lockdown regulations, we would not even be permitted to host any sort of gathering afterwards. Everything was impacted by COVID's grasp on the world.

As the hearse and other cars arrived at the crematorium. I was still in shock when my mother arrived in her coffin. It was as though everything had been a nightmare. It wasn't, though. It was real. As I waited in the car behind to follow, there she was.

I was unsure of my emotions. I was disappointed and enraged that I was never given an additional opportunity to interact with and speak to her. Given the circumstances, I'm told I shouldn't be so hard on myself. These were not ordinary circumstances. We were still in the grip of a pandemic.

When we arrived at the crematorium, one of the funeral directors stated unequivocally that she was responsible for enforcing the rules. The rules stated that only 30 people could enter, and you all had to wear masks. Everyone else would have to wait outside.

Once inside, we were told to please keep our social distance, this was reiterated as everyone made their way to the pews. My brothers and her grandsons carried her coffin into the church and laid it down as the music played. Once we were all seated, the service began.

The service was short, did not last long. The curtains were drawn after the service, and the coffin was gone. That was the end of Norma Cummings, my mother. She wasn't there anymore. I returned a few days later to collect my mother's ashes. I signed for her ashes and still could not process the previous few weeks. I was carrying her ashes in a wooden box. My mom was in this box as ashes. It was a very emotional day for all of us.

January 29, 2021

I hadn't slept well the entire time. Nothing had changed in my perimenopausal world. My hot flashes were present, but with everything else going on, I wasn't focusing on them as much. My mind was currently in the present events that I was dealing with, which were as sad as they were.

In fact, there were so many other things going on during this time that perimenopause was interrupted. There was no time to pay attention to my usual symptoms, from the moment I landed until the moment I left. Perhaps once I returned home to Canada, I would then be able to feel some sort of release from everything and get a better perspective of things. The almost three weeks we spent flew by and we would soon be leaving.

Our flights back to Canada were scheduled for January 31. Before we traveled, we needed to get our return COVID PCRs done. We arrived at the airport early this morning, paid our fees, and waited in line to get our tests. Prior to departure, we would receive our results. If they were positive, we wouldn't be able to fly anywhere. Fortunately, they returned negative, so we were free to depart on January 31. This would be a sad day when we had to leave.

January 30, 2021

My mother was no longer with us, and it was a strange yet very sad time for me and my family. Before we left, I went back by my sick aunt's house. She was relieved to see us from a distance, and I was relieved to give her one last wave. My aunt was unable to attend my mother's funeral, which must have been difficult for her. She was too vulnerable in her current situation and health.

At this point, I did not know when I would return to the U.K or if I would see my aunt again. She appeared frail and had lost weight since I saw her two years prior.

Tonight would be our last night before boarding a plane and returning to Canada. We spent the evening with family members and ate homemade lasagna prepared by my husband, which was delicious. Although the house felt empty without her presence, I couldn't understand what had happened. Her ashes were in a box in the house, and it was all too much.

I had pretty much sorted out a lot of her stuff up until this point. Once stores opened, my brother would donate many of her belongings. Because of the current lockdown, no businesses were open or accepting donations. I'm still trying to make sense of it all. Perhaps once I leave and have a moment to reflect on the last few weeks, it will then all sink in. I will not likely revisit England for a while, now that my dear mother is no longer with us. The notion of her not being there continues to feel strange.

January 31, 2021

We had to leave early to catch a flight to London. Our flight to Toronto would depart in the afternoon. We had flown to England during a pandemic, buried my mother, and waved goodbye to my sick aunt, and now we were returning, still during a pandemic.

I had conflicting emotions, and I never knew what I was feeling at the time. It had all happened so quickly, with no time to ponder the magnitude of it all. My mother had died so suddenly. It all came out of nowhere, completely unexpectedly. I question myself as to why she did not mention anything if she knew she was sick.

When we arrived in London, we had to download the Arrive Can app and double-check that all our information was correct. It was strange to see the largest signs ever seen in an airport on each seat. Maintain your distance. There were scribbles on the floor. The repeated communication coming from over the microphone, it was all so bizarre. We were reminded of the times with our continued mask wearing. It was all like something out of a film. We were about to board our flight back to Toronto and be quarantined for two weeks. Fortunately, I wasn't working; my husband was, but he'd be home for two weeks.

We arrived safely, and thankfully, neither myself nor my husband contracted COVID-19 during the journey. We were thankful for this; we were also cautious throughout our travels. By the time we arrived at our house, I was both grateful and exhausted. Fortunately, my dear friend anticipated our arrival and purchased enough groceries for us to last at least a week.

We stayed at home, and security called and came to check on us to make sure we didn't leave during the quarantine period. Even the U.K. health department called us a week later to tell us that someone on our flight from Manchester to London had tested positive. We were already back in Canada and keeping our distance. It was a long journey.

For a while, during my time away, I thought I was no longer in perimenopause. Then I remembered that everything that had happened in the previous two months had disrupted my perimenopause. But now it was time to return to reality. I just needed some time to relax and collect my thoughts.

Back in Canada

February 15, 2021

It's been a few weeks since we returned from the United Kingdom. Even though the previous month was like a whirlwind of sadness, now that we are back in Canada, I have a moment to process what happened. I didn't have time to think in England because things had to be done quickly given the circumstances. My mother was still alive a few months ago. What can I do now that she is gone?

My mind is still scattered, and I'm thinking in my head and beating myself up about it. I could have spent more time with her if I had been there sooner. Then I try to reason with my mind and remember that by the time we knew, we were experiencing a pandemic that could have had dire consequences. My mother was sick and vulnerable at the time, and she needed to be protected from infection. I hope I can accept this one day, because I can't right now. I simply hoped to spend more time with her.

Throughout my absence, all my symptoms were far from my mind. Even if they were present, I was too preoccupied with other things to think about them at the time. When I was in England, I still did not sleep well because my mother had died. I got by on little sleep and ignored my perimenopausal symptoms. There was no time to ponder these issues; now that I am back, we will see how things progress.

Hot flashes and sleepless nights continue to dominate my life, and I haven't considered any solutions or ideas to help me. I'll just keep suffering. Some days it bothers me, while others I just get on with it. I despise perimenopause and its accompanying symptoms.

February 19, 2021

I'm still stunned by what has happened over the last few months. My mother's death is fresh in my mind, and it is extremely difficult. I only have memories and pictures of my mother. She is now merely a memory.

She's gone, and I'm still in a state of shock. I'm not sure if I'll ever understand the gravity of losing my mother. Growing up, she was the prominent figure in my life, she was my rock. She will live on in my thoughts and memories, and she will never be forgotten. It is not easy as it only happened just over a month ago. It will take time Michaela, it's not easy.

February 24, 2021

Today, I learned that my uncle Peter, my mother's brother, has died of COVID-19. He was in the hospital at the same time as my mother. He'd had a fall and was admitted after Christmas. They had wheeled him down to see my mother one last time before she died while he was in the hospital.

A month later, he died with no relatives present, only a staff member. Such tragic circumstances and much like a lot of stories being heard around the world. Patients dying alone and family members were not allowed into the hospital because of the current situation. Horrific times. At least he was in the hospital and not totally alone when he passed.

Along with my mother's death, this was more heartbreaking news. Her older brother had died. She had spent a lot of time over the holidays taking care of him and making sure he was OK and had enough food before he fell.

It's been a bleak start to the year 2021. I couldn't believe I'd lost two family members in a matter of months. Another sad day would be his funeral. I'd watch his funeral service online with other viewers in a few weeks. I need to take some time and reflect on hearing all this devastating news. It does not help being in the winter. February is already a somewhat depressing time for me. Up until now I have still not had a cycle and I know soon I will be hitting the twelfth month mark without a period.

March 18, 2021

Today I watched my uncle's online memorial service. It was another heartbreaking day and loss for our family. The service was brief, and due to covid, only a small number of people were able to attend. As I watched the service, I couldn't believe my uncle had died just one month after I had lost my mother, and that I was watching his funeral online.

I'm relieved that I was able to connect to the service without interruption. I noticed that some of my family members were present. For our family, this was a difficult time filled with grief. I am grateful for technology. At the very least, it allows you to feel a part of it and see everything unfold before your eyes. I'm glad I was able to watch it; I just don't like the circumstances surrounding his death. Life can be unfair at times, especially when multiple family members die within months of each other.

Celebration Time: Come On, Let's Celebrate!

March 20, 2021

For me, today is that day. I am officially in menopause; I have not had a period for a year. Should I be happy and rejoice? I'd say it's more of a relief now not to have to deal with those monthly periods any longer. I'm not going to miss the inconvenience of it all. It's wonderful knowing, I won't have to bring any sanitary products with me when I travel. I won't have to worry about having a period at the start or end of my holiday.

All of this is good news. The time finally arrived, period-free menopause. Well, I suppose it's a start. But only time will tell if my other symptoms improve and if my sleep gets any better.

Up until this point, I've still been having problems sleeping. The hot flashes appear and disappear. Although the emphasis has not been on all my symptoms of late. Perhaps I am now entering a new phase and things will only get better. Maybe things will start to look up for me during these times. It would be amazing if the brain fog, body aches, joint pain, and sweating disappeared.

I still can't seem to embrace this time in my life, despite what some books tell me. For me, it continues to go on and on. If only it would stop. I should also stop procrastinating and try to do something for myself. My girlfriend is taking a small dosage of HRT and she says it helps her a lot. I have not got that far to think of such a thing as it seems too much effort. I know with this kind of attitude; I will just have to take everything as it comes. I just hope it's not like they say for the next ten years.

Hallelujah! Bye bye. My womanhood cycle has finished and that part of it was a relief. The symptoms and post-menopause will continue.

Spring has sprung and the pandemic is still among us.

March 25, 2021

It's been a difficult start to the year, especially with the loss of two family members. During this time, things were also not looking good for my aunty Carol (mom's sister), who was battling bowel cancer.

During the pandemic, she was in and out of the hospital, making it difficult for family members, including myself, to even be close to her. I've never experienced anything so agonizing. Being in the same country to visit a family member and not being able to see them. It was so frustrating; I only looked at her and smiled, and then we had a brief conversation. All because of the pandemic and to keep her safe from infections.

She was too vulnerable to be close to her. When she waved to me, it broke my heart. She had deteriorated significantly since the last time I saw her a few years ago. Throughout it all, she maintained a positive attitude. It was particularly distressing because this was one of my closest aunts. She was making progress, but things were not looking good. I'd spoken with my aunt a few times before, and she always seemed upbeat despite her situation.

April 3, 2021

I received a text message at 9:23 a.m. this morning informing me that my aunt had died half an hour ago in the United Kingdom. She died peacefully, surrounded by her family and friends. There are no words to describe how I feel right now.

Just another blow that has knocked me down. My aunt Carol was one of my mother's older sisters. I spent of lot of time with this aunt while growing up in England. Three family members have been taken from us in the last three months. It's hard to digest, and again I have a lump in my throat. The hardest part was not being able to hug her because of the pandemic, that had hurt. I could only stand there and watch, knowing it was probably the last time I'd see her when I was in the U.K.

The three deaths occurred within a few months of one another. This was unfortunate news. While it was expected, I didn't expect it so soon. I'm both stunned and saddened by it all. 2021 continues to be a sad time. Another blow to my family and my mother's remaining siblings. There are now only three of them left alive.

It's still difficult to process everything. My wonderful aunt was now another memory. Once again, I would not be able to attend her funeral. I would wait for details of the date so I could view it online. A sign of the times.

April 7, 2021

It was a beautiful day today, so I went for a walk to enjoy the sunshine. On a positive note, the weather is improving. I took advantage of the fact that I was able to get outside and have some sun exposure. Another stay-at-home order was on its way to Toronto. I'm still trying to comprehend the magnitude of my loss in such a short period of time. Three family members in three months.

My eyes well up with tears as I recall all of them. Because of the craziness of the times, I was never able to say my final goodbyes. Everything has made me angry, and I feel cheated. I was aware that these were not normal circumstances. COVID-19 separated us, and I was unable to support or be as close to any of them as I would have liked. It's never far from my mind. I only wish we weren't amid a pandemic because that didn't help. It's difficult to accept; it's simply not fair.

April 11, 2021

So much has occurred in such a short period of time. I haven't had time to consider my new menopausal situation. Yes, I am period-free, and what a long time it seemed. My menopause was disrupted by the recent devastating news, and I still haven't had time to process everything that has happened. My nights are consumed by thoughts of the special people I have lost.

While there are still symptoms and sleepless nights, I am not dwelling on my continued womanly troubles now. I have still not made a conscious effort to find some source of relief for my symptoms.

For now, that is not my priority. I still have another online service to watch for my aunt. Once the funeral arrangements are made, I will be notified of all the details. I was told my aunt passed peacefully surrounded by friends and family. I am happy she was not alone at the time of her passing, and she was surrounded by love at that moment.

April 21, 2021

I received a text message today informing me that my aunt would be laid to rest on April 23. The funeral would begin at 11:30 a.m., followed by the burial. I'd be able to watch the church service online and hear from my relatives about how the burial went. I was not looking forward to another online service so soon. It would be another difficult moment.

Aunty Carol's Funeral

April 23, 2021

Last night was another sleepless night, and I was sweating profusely. The covers were on and off at the same time. My thoughts were racing as I considered another funeral service for my aunt the following day. My aunty Carol celebrated her 78th birthday in February, and today was the day she was laid to rest.

My thoughts returned to my family in my home country. I would be sent a link to watch the service once more. The service lasted over an hour, and it appears that a larger number of people were permitted to attend at this time. It was a very sad moment to watch and take in, nevertheless. It was painful to watch from a distance as her grandchildren spoke on her behalf. My aunty Carol had left us. I'll miss her terribly.

At the end of the service, people would make their way to the cemetery where she would be laid to rest. Followed by a celebration of her life. More people were permitted to attend than in the previous months. Doves were released during the celebration and a song she loved was played, 'Oh Carol' by the famous Neil Sedaka. She had a good send off, as they would say back home.

May 2, 2021

Since returning from the U.K., my hot flashes have become more noticeable. They appear to be returning to the same level as before. I'm still suffering from a lack of sleep, and my body feels terrible at times. When I try to sleep, I feel terrified because my heart palpitations are ten to the dozen.

Given all the things that have happened thus far, it's no wonder. It's just been terrible. My thoughts and feelings are still all over the place right now. My own menopausal struggles continue to weigh me down, and I'm not feeling well because of the recent sad news and family deaths. I can't stand the menopause, and I'm afraid I'll never be able to sleep properly again. I just want to feel rested and as if I got a good night's sleep. It's just not happening.

This has been my story for the past year or more. The broken record is still playing out one day after another.

May 6, 2021

I awoke this morning with my usual aches and pains in my joints. This morning, I had my coffee, and I'm not sure where my sudden burst of energy came from. I feel energized, and I feel like cleaning while I'm in the mood. My days can vary from one day to the next. Like I mentioned before, I will take these good days. I only wish for more. It seems vaccines are the topic of the moment. COVID-19 is still making headlines, even though vaccines are now widely available and being administered. There appears to be some hope on the horizon.

This is positive news which we all need at this point. I'm still sleeping poorly. I still toss and turn all night and wake up drenched in sweat. There was a time when I thought my sleep was getting better. That was a wishful thought. This is my normal, which will remain for a long time. What is going on is crazy, or at least that is how it feels. I am struggling and I think I need help.

The problem is, now you cannot even get in to see a doctor, let alone talk about menopause.

May 10, 2021

It's been almost 4 months since my mother died, and every day brings back memories and sadness. Her order of service program is on top of my sideboard, and I greet it and look at it every day. I can't pick up the phone and call her anymore, which is excruciating. It feels like it was only yesterday we lost her, and I believe it will stay with me forever. It was my mother.

My eyes well up as I look at the old photographs. I'm still in shock that she's gone, and I am having a hard time believing it. Remember the saying, "You don't know what you have until it is gone."

For me, this rings true at this moment. I'm dealing with a lot mentally right now and trying to wrap my head around it all. In comparison to what some people are going through, it may seem insignificant. Even though it all bothers me, I am grateful for many other things. Yes, the stresses of post-menopause and its symptoms continue daily, with some days being better than others. Add in the pandemic and that is another mental challenge. I hope in time things will get better; I hope so.

May 21, 2021

Today, May 21, would have been my mother's 73rd birthday. I feel down. It felt strange not being able to call her and wish her a happy birthday. She wasn't there.

For years, I could at least send her my best wishes, but now I couldn't. This will take some time to adjust to on those special occasions. I can look through her photos and remember the good times.

My mother enjoyed listening to 60s music, she also liked John Holt, the reggae star. One of her favorites was "Help Me Make It Through the Night," which I've been listening to on YouTube since returning from England, along with all his other classics. On what would have been her special day, these were the memories I could only hold onto and remember.

My husband and I decided to celebrate her birthday by making a dish that she would enjoy cooking whenever we visited her in England. She always made Spaghetti Bolognese pasta with garlic bread. My husband, who is Italian, always appreciated her British-style dishes. It is now nothing more than a memory, and that is all we have.

Although I believe you can never truly recover from the loss of a parent, it is still extremely painful. I'm hoping that it gets easier with time. On May 27, it would have been my uncle Peter's birthday and sadly he is also no longer with us. Just the thought of the last few months continues to be a struggle and angers me so much.

May 30, 2021

Since losing my mother, I've been replaying the events that led up to that first text from my brother in December

2020. I can't get those images of her lying in bed nearing the end of her life in the hospital when we arrived out of my head. Every day, I'm sad and angry because there wasn't enough time. She knew we were there, but it wasn't enough. The circumstances were terrible; I only wish I could have been there sooner. I just keep trying to make sense of it all. Bloody pandemic!

June 2, 2021

As we head into the warmer months, the pandemic is still here. I am still going for my walks, but usually in the morning. I am still fighting with post-menopausal stuff, sleep, aches, and pains. I am still watching my travel shows on YouTube and doing my workouts. I am keeping socially distant or in my bubble.

I am still just following the guidelines as best as I can. Right now, I am still not currently employed, and I am thankful for this. I am not sure I could cope mentally and physically with my ongoing struggles, hot flashes, migraines and more in a work setting. I do not know how women manage.

June 25, 2021

The COVID pandemic continues, and some people worldwide have received one or two doses of the vaccine. Some people have also died because of vaccine-related complications. There are also antivaxxers who will never take it. It's been 5 months since my mother died, and it still hurts and seems strange. I can only continue to look at pictures and curse the pandemic to myself. If we hadn't been going through this, I could have seen her and supported her.

I've been told not to beat myself up about it. We are in the grip of a pandemic. She's no longer here; she's gone, and everything is still unsettling. I believe her loss will linger for a long time. I find it more difficult each day.

When I returned to Canada, I brought a few sentimental items with me. Such as perfume, clothing items, and a few other mementos. These will assist me in keeping her close by, reminding me of her, and feeling her presence with me. I will always cherish my memories because they cannot be taken away from me.

I recall my mother buying me my first record player. It had flashing disco lights, and I remember listening to single records. My favorite records were *Never knew love like this before* by Stephanie Mills and *Upside Down* by Diana Ross. I adored my little player, and this is one of many wonderful memories I have of her. I was ecstatic at that time, just the thought of it brought tears to my eyes.

As we head into the warmer months, the pandemic is still here. I am still going for my walks, but usually in the morning. Despite my ongoing issues, I continue to walk, watch my shows, and exercise when I can. I also keep listening to the current guidelines.

June 29, 2021

As each day passes, I have my good and bad days. I'm going up and down with it all. The pandemic, post-menopause, and midlife. Sometimes I feel so low. Then there's my ongoing dieting battle. I feel like I'm still fighting with food after twenty years. Some weeks are a struggle, while others are a little easier. When I indulge, I always feel so bad about myself.

Given that the last six months have been difficult since my mother's death, I sometimes feel like I'm repeating the same old cycle with no control. At times, I continue to eat mindlessly and feel terrible afterwards. When will it be over? I know I'm the only one who can control my eating habits. At my age, I need to be more self-aware, given all the health concerns that come with being 50 plus.

July 7, 2021

It's one of those weeks when my eating habits and temptation seem to be winning. Why can't I just say no to chocolate and sugary treats? At times I feel as if I am still going to have my menstrual cycle, but I am in menopause. Fortunately, this week my hot flashes appear to be decreasing in frequency, which is a good sign.

When these days come, I continue to rejoice. I'm still not making a concerted effort to do or take something for relief. Maybe I'm just tired at this point. I'll just whine and complain and put up with it all. Only I can make the change. I am the type of person who would rather suffer. Unless there is a miracle cure for my night sweats and terrible sleep, I will continue to bear it all after nearly two years.

Another concern has been that, given my family history with various cancers, I feel I don't want to increase my risk by taking pills, even if they may aid me. I will just continue to try and do my best with diet and exercise.

I was thinking a lot about my mother today. I'm still furious about the pandemic. I'm still sorry for not being there earlier and spending that time with her.

July 8, 2021

With millions of deaths, COVID-19 continues to dominate the news. Vaccines, variants, and herd immunity appear to be buzzwords right now. I can't take it any longer, no matter how much I try. There are still some days that are mentally tough. The only thing that's also helping right now is that it is summer, and a sunny day can lift my spirits.

Another good distraction from the current situation has been the European soccer games. It is something to sort of be excited about. I mean something that the entire world can watch and cheer for instead of listening to and watching the pandemic's ongoing nightmare. We can focus on sports, which are always fun to watch. I will enjoy watching the euro cup final between England and Italy on July 11. "Come on England!" There will be me cheering for England and my Italian husband cheering for his team.

Not only are the Euros in play, but the fan-less Olympics will begin this month. Unfortunately, due to the covid situation, they were unable to take place last year. The games will also serve as a pleasant diversion from the current situation. Although it will be different from previous years, I am confident it will be entertaining and a welcome distraction from our current situation.

European Final
Come On, England!

July 11, 2021

People had gathered to watch the football game. While some countries' rules remained stricter than others, it was great to see crowds again. Due to the outbreak, large sporting events, concerts, and other large gatherings have been prohibited for the past year or so. This was clearly a sign of hope. It was inspiring to see people cheering for their country amid a pandemic. Whoever won or lost, this was something to see, and there was a lot of excitement surrounding this final.

At Wembley Stadium, it appeared as if there had been no pandemic. People had come out to watch the football game. With sixty thousand people in the stands, the game was decided on penalties. Italy missed two, while England missed three. Some England fans acted like losers, hurling racial epithets at the players who missed the penalties for England.

As a British person, it can be embarrassing to hear about the fans and how they behave when they lose a game. Italy defeated England in the 2020 Euro cup final. As far as I am concerned, the English team was amazing to even get to the final. More positivity would be nice. At least, the Euros were a nice diversion from the doom and gloom. In a few weeks, we will see a very different Olympics with no fans. During these current times, sports are always a great escape.

July 18, 2021

Last night was another sleepless night, I was soaking wet and did my usual tossing and turning. I was feeling quite emotional this morning. When I looked at pictures of my mother, still wondering why she had to leave. I then recall the pandemic and am always enraged that I never saw her in better shape or alertness before she left us.

It replays in my head all the time. How the events unfolded and how fast she went. Within two weeks, and that was it, she was gone. She was not going to come back, and I cannot even pick up the phone now. She is not there. Although I continue with my day-to-day life, life is not the same anymore without her.

July 21, 2021

I awoke today feeling as if I'd been hit by a bus. I felt dizzy as well. I dislike this stage of my life. It's terrible, and I can't seem to accept it. Surprisingly, my hot flashes have been minimal this month, but the soaking night sweats have returned, and my insomnia has persisted. That is an endless story.

I'm completely exhausted. I'm still putting off using any products that might help. Instead, I'm dealing with it all and suffering. There always seems to be a lot to deal with. I just wish I was so much more knowledgeable about it all. It may have prepared me a little better, and I could have studied and researched it all.

Now is not really a good time for me to start further research, I haven't paid it too much thought to be honest. My mind is consumed with grief and the pandemic at this moment. I am still trying to keep safe and not catch COVID. Meanwhile, the ongoing banter around variants and COVID-19 continues.

August 29, 2021

Another restless night with fragmented sleep. I awoke this morning with my second finger swollen. I started researching on the internet and read different theories about what it could be.

It really is all about ailments. At least the hot flashes subsided a bit in July, even though the night sweats were rough. I suppose when all this is happening, you cannot have it all. As I am discovering, there is always some sort of symptom. I'm looking forward to the long weekend in September.

With travel options still limited, I believe that staying close to home is the best choice right now. There are still numerous variants floating around. I don't think I could handle the hassle of traveling overseas again for a while. Although a real vacation would be ideal, I am willing to wait until things improve.

Labor Day—Long Weekend

September 1, 2021

We were getting ready to drive a few hours to our vacation home as Labor Day approached. My husband expressed he didn't feel good while driving. He assumed it was simply because he was tired from work or because of his diabetes. We decided to pull over on the way so he could rest and eat something. His blood sugar level could have been low.

Neither myself nor my husband had previously contracted COVID-19. We were always concerned about him being diabetic and thus more vulnerable during the pandemic. He always wears his mask at work, and we've mostly stayed in our own social bubble. We had not been mixing and had kept our distance. Fortunately, following all the rules and guidelines had kept us safe.

We continued to our destination after he finished his sandwich. When we arrived, he went straight to bed, thinking he'd feel better in the morning. During the night, he felt like he had a fever, and so the next morning we decided to go and buy a COVID rapid test.

September 2, 2021

Given that I spent the entire time in the car with him, we each paid for a test. If he was sick, I would pick up whatever he had. When we got our results, his test came back positive and mine came back negative. Given the rumors about the dependability of these drugstore tests, it was not looking good. We then went to a walk-in clinic to be retested.

However, we would have to wait until the next day to learn of our results. We returned home and planned to stay there until we received our results. I felt fine at the time; I wasn't experiencing any of the symptoms he was experiencing. Rest would be the best thing to do and hope for a quick recovery if it was indeed COVID-19.

He continued to not feel great and once again he retired to his bed early as he just felt pretty wiped out. At this moment, though, he was not experiencing any respiratory issues, which was a relief. Especially after watching the ongoing respiratory problems in the world related to COVID-19.

September 3, 2021

We were called around noon by a public health officer who informed us that Ippolito, my husband, had tested positive for the coronavirus and needed to isolate. I was negative, but because I was in close contact, I would have to isolate myself and return several times to be retested. He had to be quarantined for 14 days. He had already started to feel ill a few days before. He did not have any energy or his usual appetite and went to bed for a lie down.

Throughout the night, he developed a fever and felt woozy. We had avoided this dreadful disease up until this point. It had finally caught up with one of us, despite our efforts to remain vigilant and adhere to protocols. We were trying to figure out how he got it. He was wearing his mask during his working hours, and it's possible he caught it from one of his coworkers who had removed his mask and was close to him.

He was unsure, however. He simply did not feel well. Sanitizer was used again, and masks were worn even in our own home. We kept our distance from each other most of the time.

My first thoughts were that it was strange that I had not tested positive, even though we had been together the entire time. This messed up our escape, but at least we were at home and could isolate. Inside, we wore masks and slept in separate quarters. I made dinner for us, but he wasn't feeling well and had lost his appetite. Pretty much for the rest of the day, he remained in his room. I would prepare something light to eat.

Later that evening, he came down but continued to feel wiped out. He had a little soup and a few crackers and returned to his bed.

September 5, 2021

I was told to test again today and to expect my results the next day. My results were negative and remained negative for the rest of the times I was tested. Meanwhile, my husband was sick with a fever, chills and was sleeping a lot. He had lost his sense of smell and was unwilling to eat. Fortunately, we were able to isolate ourselves and remain socially distant from one another.

I never caught the virus, which was a huge relief. The virus, on top of my menopausal symptoms, would have been too much for me. I'm already going through a stressful time in my life, and I didn't want the added stress of COVID-19. We were grateful he was able to recover and thought about all those who were not so fortunate in their recovery. It was a challenging moment for us both, even though only he was the one dealing with the symptoms.

September 14, 2021

My husband had a rough week, but he remained strong throughout his bout with covid. Even though he was exhausted, lethargic and had lost his appetite. He eventually regained his energy and was able to rekindle his appetite. During these times, thank goodness for grocery delivery and medication delivery.

Given our circumstances, they were extremely beneficial, and we gratefully acknowledged their assistance. It was also difficult for my husband to be confined to the house because he enjoys working, and this setback meant he could only rest and not do anything else. Though we were confined to our home, we thankfully have an outdoor space which we were able to make use of. When you have covid, being able to sit outside in the summer is a blessing and he could remain socially distant.

September 20, 2021

I was extremely fortunate not to have contracted COVID-19. While I was aware of my husband's situation, we were cautious at the time. My menopausal symptoms were brushed aside during the weeks of isolation because I was concerned about my husband's well-being and taking care of his needs, given how he felt. Nonetheless, he made a good recovery, for which we are grateful.

October 2, 2021

I decided to go out and get some Swiss HRT supplements today. It had taken a long time, but I finally made the effort today. I had read reviews and, as with anything, different products work differently for different people. I had read both positive and negative reviews.

At this point, I'd have to give them a shot and see if they could help me. Maybe they could help me get through my menopause craziness. My sleep is the real issue I need assistance with it. While I manage my sweats and flashes and try to get on with my life, it's the sleep and those mornings when I wake up feeling like I've been hit by a truck. I am an impatient person who prefers to see results quickly. This applies to any type of supplement or tablet I take. Usually, you need time to see results.

October 7, 2021

It's a new month, and you never know what can happen in a new month. My post-menopause nightmares persist. The winter is approaching and that is not always a pleasant feeling to bear. Winters in Canada can feel like an eternity, especially if the snow comes early.

I was feeling down this morning as I stared out the window. Up until this day, my moods had been stable. Of course, I didn't sleep last night, but in my world, that's nothing new. Then a suicidal thought entered my mind. I'm not sure where this train of thought came in. Just like that, I was feeling depressed and sad. I was lost and staring outside the window at the bare trees. I had no control over these thoughts.

I tried to figure out why I was suddenly thinking like this. The sensation came from nowhere. My mind was scattered throughout the day, and I just kept thinking and feeling down. The day progressed and by the end of it, I felt a little better. In an instant, my mind and feelings switched.

That was a strange feeling; I hadn't felt that low since I was in my perimenopausal stage. That thought changed quickly. Overall, even though I continue to struggle daily, that feeling came out of nowhere. I am happy to say it is not a frequent occurrence and it soon waned away.

October 8, 2021

Today, I feel better than I did yesterday. I'm not sure where that feeling came from; it was completely unexpected. I started crying as those horrifying thoughts entered my mind. It was as if I had fallen into this dark hole and was struggling to climb out. Why does all of this seem so difficult to deal with?

It is undoubtable that I was not prepared for anything like this. I am happy that each of my days are not met like this. Even when I approached the perimenopause, there was no talk or direction. Just a quick, "Oh, you're in menopause," and that's all.

The only thing that has helped me is reading up on things on the internet. It's mostly the same stuff said by different people. HRT, diet and exercise. Is it fabulous to be fifty? I don't think so. Or, at the very least, I can speak for myself, and it does not appear to be the case.

I know I'm not the only one going through it; all women around the world are and will continue to go through it. All our symptoms will be unique. While some women may not experience any symptoms at all. I wish I could be one of those women.

Sleepless nights and all my other symptoms continue.

November 8, 2021

I haven't noticed any significant difference after one month of taking Swiss HRT supplements. But I should give it a try for a few months. Time and patience, I believe, will be required here. I simply want immediate results, and to be honest, I am not optimistic. I'll give it some time. Don't be so negative, Michaela.

There is a lot of change going on in my midlife. Things seemed to be going along fine until the onset of perimenopause and menopause. Now I'm starting to notice differences in my overall appearance. Physical changes have been taking place for some time.

Overall, the change appears to be drastic at times, and I don't like what I see on some days. I'm beginning to pay closer attention. When I looked at my phone's reflection today, I saw a turkey neck. I needed to take another look, and as I got a closer look, I didn't like what I saw. "Oh, that looks terrible," I thought to myself. Seeing the reflection made me stop in my tracks.

After all this time looking in the mirror, I had never really paid attention to my neck. My neck was the focus now. My first thoughts were, I need to get some neck cream. I dislike getting older, even more now that I am noticing all these physical changes. Neck cream will be on my shopping list yet again. Whenever I get around to purchasing it.

Now that I'm in my fifties, the signs of ageing are becoming apparent. I recall hearing comments about getting old and reaching a certain age, with the implication that "it's all downhill from here." I understand what people are saying. On the other hand, I suppose it could be your perception of ageing and how you see it.

One thing is for sure, though, you should be kind to yourself. Your body deserves love and self-care. I know being proactive with your health is important and I can attest to that even more in my midlife. Sometimes trying to be kind is met with the negativity on occasions. On my thighs again, when I get out of the shower, I start to see the ripples of cellulite, but I just kind of ignore it, I know it is there to stay.

It is so funny how right up until my fifties, I never noticed any of these things and suddenly they are just there in my face. I don't mind wrinkles, but I do notice my face changing and the nasolabial folds are prominent as I glance in the mirror. Perhaps I'll have to find some facial exercises to make the folds less noticeable. I've never considered cosmetic surgery. I don't think I'd be interested in going this route.

That is not for me. Although it works for some women. Everyone is free to do whatever makes them feel better about themselves. Things change as we age, including our facial appearance; perhaps acceptance also helps. I'm getting older, and it's all part of the process, just try to be graceful with it and what works for you.

November 28, 2021

Another month has passed, and despite taking the supplements for nearly two months, I am still not seeing a significant improvement in symptoms. I believe that once I have completed my second batch of supplements, I will not accept any more. My joints have been aching a lot lately.

While I am grateful to wake up each day and move, I can become stiff at times. Maybe if I had a regular workout routine, I wouldn't be as stiff or achy on some days. I'm an on-again, off-again exerciser, and staying motivated has been more difficult in the winter, even when I'm at home. As the year nears the end, I reflect on how much I miss my mother.

As we enter the month of December, it will be a difficult one. There isn't a day that goes by that I don't think of her and how quickly she was taken away. I frequently come to a halt and reflect on the tragic event. We were trapped by the pandemic. I wish I could have spent more time with her, just more time when she was present and not out of it.

When I recall that moment, it makes me sad and brings tears to my eyes. My mother's order of service and a chain with her ashes remain out so I can view them. I can't take it down yet because I'm not ready. It still feels like it happened yesterday. I just need to keep my strength and faith and keep going. Life goes on, and I am grateful that my mother is no longer in pain.

Sometimes all I want to do is pick up the phone and say hello. Even though our discussions were brief, I miss hearing her voice on the other end of the phone. She became ill around this time last year, but she was still with us. I'm not feeling the Christmas spirit this year; I'm feeling down, and I just want it to pass quickly. Once the year is over, I can try to be a little more optimistic and hope that 2022 will be a better year.

Merry Christmas!

December 25, 2021

This Christmas will be low-key, as I am not in the mood for festivities. It has been a difficult year to cope with all the events that have occurred. In the back of my mind, I know December will continue to be a mental challenge. I remember what happened a year ago and where I was when I received the news. I knew she'd be on my mind during the holidays, as well as the other family members we lost.

I think back to my childhood and how she made our Christmases so memorable as children, there were always plenty of presents under the tree. Including brand new clothes, toys and selection boxes containing my favorite Cadburys British chocolate. This Christmas, I couldn't pick up the phone because she wasn't there.

Even though I left the U.K. many years ago, I always spoke to my mother on special occasions, such as Christmas. Even though we were far apart, having a phone line for communication was extremely convenient. Technology was always useful for me when I needed to FaceTime her.

When I returned from the United Kingdom, I brought back some of my mother's clothing. A beautiful red Christmas jumper. I wore her sweater today to be close to her and feel her presence. I was sad and wished she was still there. It hurts a lot, but I know her memories will live on and never fade. She was my mother, and despite our distance, I adored her.

During this time, we are still exercising caution considering the ongoing covid situation and remaining socially distant in a sense. My mental health has surely changed over the past few years with the events that have happened. At some point though, life must go on.

New Year, New World: Happy 2022!

January 1, 2022

We're still talking about COVID-19 in waves, and I doubt it will ever stop. Yes, there is still covid in the air, and I am sure the entire world is sick of hearing the same record that has been playing for a few years now. It just doesn't seem to end. You can't get away from it at times, as current reminders remain from wearing a mask to stickers on the floor. The ongoing discussion of vaccines and cases. Will this ever be over? With restrictions in some countries being lifted, it seems people are trying to move forward and resume normal life.

Monkey pox is the latest new virus that has emerged, fortunately not as fatal as covid, which is a relief, and there hasn't been much talk about it, which is also a good thing. Cases have emerged here and there, but covid continues to dominate the airwaves. Covid fatigued is what the world is feeling at this point, including myself and my husband.

It's been almost two and a half years since we traveled for a vacation, and up until this point, I thought I couldn't be bothered with all the hassle of travel. I didn't want to deal with crowded airports and chaos. Masks are still required to be worn on the plane.

I'm exhausted just thinking about it. People are traveling now, however; I believe that enough time has passed and that, after the sheer exhaustion of covid, vacations are much needed. It's just been so long that I forgot what it was like to simply get up and leave. That appears to be an excessive amount of effort. I'm sure we'll need to get away soon.

January 13, 2022

My mother died one year ago today. It was an emotional day, and my mind was elsewhere in the United Kingdom. The year has gone by quickly, and things aren't getting any better. I miss my mother dearly. I recall exactly where I was, when she passed, and everything comes back to me so vividly as if it was yesterday.

We had sat in the hospital room and watched her slip away from us. It is still excruciatingly painful. Grief is strange; I live each day thinking about her. While I just plod along, everything appears to be fine. In a moment of thought, I can be reminded of her in some way and tears fill my eyes. She is no longer here. Life is not the same without my mother and it is going to take time to adjust, it is not easy.

A new year and there has been no change in my midlife situation. It is still there in existence and symptoms are as prevalent as they were in the last few years. I have still not made a conscious effort to make a change. So, until I do, I should not continue to whine; however, I do. I just cannot seem to bring myself to continue HRT supplements. Even if some people rave about them, I am still not convinced. That is just me.

April 2022

My girlfriends and I are still talking about menopause, and I expect it to be a topic for the rest of my life. "Just get over it." For the last few years, my vocabulary has included: hot flashes, night sweats, aching joints and bones, muffin top, brain fog, emotional roller-coaster, gray hair, turkey neck, nasolabial folds, cellulite, mood swings, sleepless nights, covers on, covers off, suicidal thoughts, feeling low, down, at the end of the road, mortality, HRT, vaginal dryness, supplements, diet, health and well-being, muscle mass, bone density, colonoscopy, pap test. Can anyone relate?

We just have these common problems. At times, it feels like you're fighting a losing battle with no end in sight. My record has not changed in nearly three years, and I have simply accepted that this is how my life will be for the next ten years. I'm still on the fence about taking anything.

Although my moods haven't been too bad emotionally, I started feeling very low and suicidal again at the beginning of this month. I was just staring out the window, not feeling well. I'm not sure how or where this sudden thought came from, but it was there, and I was thinking about it again.

These thoughts lingered for several hours. I awoke the next day and went about my normal day, and I was fine. What exactly is going on in my head? Is it the menopause that is causing these horrible thoughts in me?

I've never experienced true depression. My moods were all over the place earlier in the perimenopausal stage, and I felt so low at times, like I had no control. But the most recent episodes appeared out of nowhere. I told my girlfriend about it, and she said that she has also experienced such lows where it felt like she could not control her thoughts.

May 2022

Today, May 21, would have been my mother's 74th birthday. Like the previous birthday, we celebrated with a nice Italian meal. She is still present in my thoughts, and I know she always will be. As I try to move on without her, she is there to guide me. I'm now in the throes of post-menopause. Neither mother, aunts, nor her friends, as far as I recall, ever discussed such matters. There was no mention of hot flashes or night sweats or anything.

For a long time, it seemed to be a taboo subject that was never discussed. Her generation made no mention of any of it. They simply got on with it, and that was it. But how could I have known? I was too young to hear about these things. The only negative association with menopause that I can remember was a simple statement and nothing more: "I think she's on the change," or "She's gone a bit funny, her."

The last two years have been an emotional roller-coaster for me, with losses and sadness. As we continue to navigate life, I continue with my own womanly journey. I'm still plodding along and haven't made any attempts to change anything. At this rate, it will be finished by the time I take any action.

After nearly a few years of living in fear because of the pandemic, the time has come to get away from it all. The last time we traveled was not for a vacation in 2021. After much deliberation and consideration, we decided to return to Italy. We had a reason to go.

On this occasion, my brother-in-law was not doing too well, which was part of the reason for our visit. I used to enjoy traveling, but I haven't felt the same way since my last trip to the U.K. after my mother died. I am confident that I would appreciate and enjoy this trip once I arrived in Italy.

Although restrictions seem more open now, my last travel was during lockdown, so I hoped this trip would be at least somewhat different. I knew COVID-19 was still present, but not on the same scale as when I had previously traveled. Though masks were still required on planes, almost all rules had been relaxed in Europe, and people were traveling more than ever.

After spending so much of this pandemic locked up, it appeared that the world had had enough. It was time to start living again. I wasn't even excited about traveling, I was more concerned about the chaos. The one advantage of traveling now is that I don't have to worry about being interrupted by my monthly or having to lug around sanitary products, which is a win and the only win during this period so far.

Italy!

June 2022

My husband had left for the trip ahead of me, and he planned to spend time with his brother before I arrived. He described the airport in Toronto as a nightmare, but he eventually got through and boarded his delayed flight. *Oh no,* I thought, *I don't want to go through all of this.*

The mere thought of it all was making me nervous. I think as I have gotten older, flying has made me feel more anxious and worried. Back in my twenties or thirties, I never thought twice about jumping on a plane off to an exotic destination.

Now it is another story. I do it because I must and it's the only way I will get to that overseas destination. I am just hoping my panic attacks don't reoccur while traveling. Although I have gotten better over time, I can still get panicked on occasions. Added to my current post-menopausal mayhem and that's a total disaster. Breathe, Michaela.

Panic Attack

My panic attacks started some years ago and came from an incident in an elevator. It all started in the blink of an eye. One day, I was riding the elevator to the second floor. I pressed the floor I wanted as soon as I entered the elevator, but nothing happened. It only took a few seconds for this panic to hit me. I abruptly lost control. I was alone, and there was no one to help me. I pressed the help button quickly, and I told the speaker, "Help, I'm stuck, and the elevator isn't moving."

I proceeded to press several buttons while still in panic mode. Then a miracle occurred, and the door opened. I quickly got out of the elevator. The issue was that I still needed to go upstairs. I'll wait for more people to board and ride along with them, I thought. So, I waited, and thankfully, people came, and I took the elevator with them to my floor. That was a huge relief.

So that would be the start of my anxiety/panic attacks, including when flying. My world changed after that incident. I became afraid to get in the elevator alone. My new world of thought. My mind wandered to panic, overthinking various situations and, at times, feeling claustrophobic.

Who would have guessed what a few seconds of confinement could do? Getting in a two-door car, riding alone on an elevator, taking the subway, and boarding a plane took a lot of thought. That sense of entrapment drove me insane for years.

I'd been going about my normal routine for quite some time after the elevator incident. I was on my way to downtown Toronto for an event. I walked down to the subway station. It was summer, and the subway train was quite crowded. I got into the car, and we started moving southbound. The train became more crowded as we passed through two stations. I was standing between a lot of people.

When we arrived at Davisville station, the train came to a halt. "We are currently experiencing issues, and the train will not be moving," the voice over the speaker said.

I was terrified at the time. I couldn't breathe, and all I could think about was getting off the train. I had to fight my way out of the train, fortunately the doors remained open. The weather was humid and hot. I felt relieved as I approached the escalator. I was now at street level and could breathe again.

The claustrophobia of the subway had vanished. I'd just freaked out and lost control. I walked further south before taking the bus to my destination. My event was taking place in the penthouse, so I would need to take another elevator. I would just need to wait for other people to take the elevator. I couldn't get into an elevator on my own any longer.

While waiting for the elevator, no one seemed to be approaching it; however, I decided to be patient. After about 7 minutes, I noticed a lady approaching me. *Yes*, I thought, *I could now enter*. She waited for the door to open. When it did, the lady entered, and so did I.

"What floor are you going to?" she inquired.

"I'm going to the penthouse," I said. Oh my god, she pressed the button for the seventh floor. I needed to go to the penthouse.

After some small talk, I expressed my apprehension about riding the elevator alone. She graciously offered to accompany me to the penthouse. I used to have the same problem, she described. I explained that it was all in my head. Yes, she said, a little cognitive therapy might help. I agreed to look into it. When we arrived at my floor, I was grateful for her presence in the elevator. Going down would not be so bad because there would be many people leaving at the same time. Phew, I'd just go with them.

Vacation Day!

June 16, 2022

My flight was scheduled to leave Toronto at 9:00 p.m. and land in Lamezia Terme, Southern Italy, at noon the next day. I scheduled my limo for 5:15 p.m. to ensure I arrived at the airport three hours before my flight. Living in Toronto, you never know what might happen on the highway, especially during rush hour. I was nervous about what to expect at the airport, as I always am before traveling. Then there were my panic attacks and claustrophobic thoughts. I simply needed to remain calm.

Where has that brave traveler vanished to? I'm now a nervous fifty-something-year-old traveler hoping to arrive safely at my destination. With my menopausal symptoms en-route, let's hope it's not too hot and the flight is smooth. When I arrived at the airport, there was a massive line. *Oh no*, I thought to myself.

I'm pretty sure I'll be here forever. But, to my surprise, the line moved quickly. There were numerous counters open. It was a simple process, checking in my bags, and before I knew it, I was sitting at my gate with time to kill. What a relief, I was expecting a headache like my husband had had the week before. Traveling alone gives me the opportunity to board the plane near the end, almost as the last person. Then, once seated, I'll fasten my belt and hope to take off quickly.

That way, I won't have to worry about being claustrophobic and having a panic attack. I know it's all in my head. My husband wants to be the first on the plane and sit for nearly an hour watching everyone else board. He claims it's to find an overhead space for the luggage. But I'm not having that.

There will be no argument about this at the airport today. I'll be the last passenger on the plane. I went to my seat after boarding the plane and sat. I wore my mask and brought sanitizer. The situation appeared to be slightly better. I arrived safely at my destination and was greeted at the airport by my husband and nephew. As usual, the Italian summer heat welcomed me outside. It was great to be back in Italy!

Let's see how I handle the heat and my hot flashes over the next two weeks. I had arrived, and now I hoped to unwind. This break was much needed, and it felt great. It was just over an hour's drive from the airport to my husband's hometown. Everything was green, and the little houses and villages nestled within the hillsides were stunning as always.

We'd spend most of our time in my husband's small town, with a four-day trip to the Amalfi coast in the middle of my two-week vacation. This time of year, in Italy was hot as usual. The question was whether I'd be able to handle the heat.

SALERNO—Amalfi coast, here we come!

June 22-26, 2022
So far, the weather has been wonderful, and the funny thing is that I was unconcerned about symptoms or anything

else. Perhaps the change in air and environment was beneficial to me.

We drove for three hours and stayed in a nice little pensione in Salerno with a sea view and a small terrace. Given the last two years of what the entire world had gone through with the global pandemic, it felt good to be away on holiday. Lazy days at the beach, eating out late in the evening and having a stroll lungo mare (stroll along the seafront) at night. Latte macchiato, a cornetto, pasta, pizza, and the splendors of Italian cuisine. I love Italy!

We chose Salerno as our base and planned to visit Capri one day and Ischia the next. We left our car at the hotel because finding a parking spot would have been difficult. For our first day trip to Capri, we would board a boat early in the morning. We kept our masks on board the boat because it was packed with tourists, and it felt safer for us.

We would stop in Amalfi, Positano, and Capri where we disembarked for the day. The island was crowded and hot, but it was wonderful to see tourists in their droves on this beautiful island and back in this beautiful country. We began our day with a latte macchiato and a nice vanilla cornetto and simply enjoyed the moment. We sat and people watched, it was thrilling to see tourism resume its full swing. Italy was one of the hardest hit countries at the start of the pandemic. It was good to see it alive again, Mama Mia!

We spent the day being tourists and trying to avoid the oppressive heat. I was engrossed in the moment of being here, browsing boutiques as well as watching tourists savor the exquisite Italian restaurants while mulling over their menus.

The world was alive again, people were laughing, and it didn't feel the same as it had the previous year. There were times when I felt like I was on fire and had hot flashes, but I tried to brush them off or wipe my face and neck as they occurred. The heat didn't help, but I was on holiday, and I was in Capri!

We returned by boat to Salerno and our lovely pensione at the end of our day. It was a lovely boat ride back, stopping to let people off in Positano and Amalfi, trying to capture the most picturesque spots from our boat. I was completely at ease. I'm grateful for this opportunity to simply enjoy my boat ride.

Our trip to the island of Ischia was equally beautiful, albeit on a much hotter day. The temperature had risen a lot. After the world came to a halt, we felt liberated and ready to enjoy travel again.

So far, my menopausal symptoms have appeared to be manageable. I wasn't overthinking my symptoms or focusing on the hot flashes; instead, I felt like I was just enjoying the moment. My sleep seemed to be slightly better than when I was in Toronto. It had to have been the Italian air, as well as being in holiday mode and in a more relaxed state of mind.

When we returned to my husband's hometown, the temperature would be over forty degrees for the next 4 days and it eventually got even hotter. Having been a sunworshipper in the past, I loved the heat. With age not so much, I embraced being indoors and not in the extreme heat. It was extremely hot during the day, making it difficult to be outside. The best times to venture out were early in the morning or late in the evening.

In any case, this was the norm in Italy in the summer. It is a norm I had become accustomed to having traveled to Italy for many years. Just everything about the place, eating out late at night, enjoying a nice pizza or pasta dish, followed by gelato and a stroll through the piazza to walk it all off. It was truly la dolce vita (the sweet life).

Before we knew it, we were packing our belongings to return to Canada, and our vacation was over. Even though COVID-19 was no longer making headlines, during our visit it appeared that cases were on the rise. While some people continued to wear masks, others did not. At this point, it is entirely up to the individual. Cases had risen further by the time we left Italy. The pandemic that shook the world was still visible in some way.

Overall, our journey was enjoyable; however, masks and the Arrive Can app were required for our return flight. We were able to enjoy ourselves for two weeks and spend time with family covid free, which was a blessing. My symptoms subsided during my vacation, which felt great. For a time, I thought life was returning to normal times. They seem to have reappeared with a vengeance once my routine was restarted.

September 18.
R.I.P Massimo De Rose.

September 2022
Sadly, my brother-in-law passed away on September 18, 2022. Only a few months after, we paid a visit to Italy. Although I was anxious about the trip, I felt some comfort knowing I was able to see him and spend some time with

him on the last occasion. We were not expecting this so soon, he was young and such a beautiful person. We will miss him dearly.

December 2022

It will be almost two years since I said goodbye to my mother in January. It was a devastating loss for my family, as well as other family members who died soon after. I miss them terribly, especially around the holidays and birthdays. They are constantly on my mind, and I am still enraged by the circumstances surrounding their deaths. I know it's something I'll have to deal with in the future. It's still very raw at times, and it's difficult to accept that's how it was during those terrible times.

Any news on Covid triggers far too many painful memories. Another year has come and gone, and it has been an eventful one. While the covid pandemic rages on, there is no end in sight. It appears to be with us for the foreseeable future. With new cases on the rise in China, some countries have reinstated the requirement for a negative covid test prior to entry.

At this point, fatigue would be an understatement for the subject of COVID-19. It's still there, but we've learned to live with it and adapt to it based on what we know.

Happy New Year 2023!

Where has the year gone? It seemed like only yesterday we ushered in 2022. Another year has passed, and I am still pretty much in the same place as when my perimenopausal journey started. Ahhhh! But that is OK because in 2023 I will be more on it.

I haven't had a physical doctor's appointment since 2019. Although, I continue to try to stay on top of my health checks and routine tests. I'm still envious of all the women who have mild to no symptoms and wish I was one of the minority groups myself. I'm gradually coming to terms with the fact that this is a stage in my life. It hasn't been an easy transition, especially since I haven't taken anything to help with my symptoms. I ask myself, is being fifty-something that old? Perhaps it is simply a matter of attitude and perspective.

I understand that age is merely a number, but why does society and everything revolve around it? In your fifties and beyond, I feel like you're done, finished, too old, and washed up, especially if you're a woman. Or at least that is how it is perceived and reported in the media and through marketing.

There are just so many visual flaws that we can't look past them. When marketing to our fifty-something age group, there is always something we should buy to avoid looking older. Wrinkle cream, menopause supplements, and cosmetic procedures like botox, liposuction facial lifts are all available. I mean, it's limitless. Why can't we just age gracefully without all this pressure when a woman reaches her "sell by date," as they call it?

We all know it's ageism at its finest, dismissing women based on their age, race, gender, or appearance in general. Rather than celebrating all of us, regardless of our age, shape, size, color, gender, or grayish or white hair. Youth is not on our side for a lifetime; we age daily, and there is nothing wrong with ageing.

Although it has its own set of challenges that I am learning to deal with, it is all part of life. Dealing with all the symptoms and so on is unpleasant at times, but it is not the end of the world. It is life. At the very least, age brings experience, confidence, and a don't-give-a-damn attitude. It simply means accepting cellulite, turkey neck, wrinkles, stiff joints, aches, and pains, and all the changes that come with age.

I'm no longer that body conscious twenty-something-year-old lying on the beach; time has passed, and I have learned to accept it, warts, and all.

As I continue my post-menopausal journey, I have learned to be my own advocate because my health matters. I am not a doctor, but I am now trying to do what works for me as well as educate myself. I have made progress if you can call it that. I have managed to get an appointment at a menopause clinic, which is often up to a year's wait. I had to ask my doctor for a referral, but it's a start for me. I am hoping to see if there is something that can help me and finally procrastination aside, I will find out.

We need more experts in this field who can guide women, so we don't just have to suffer in silence. I know there is a negative connotation around this subject and that is how I viewed it myself. Let's be real, women go through it all perimenopause, menopause, and post-menopause.

Although our journeys may be different, we should still have access to education a long time before we reach this stage. I am seeing that diet, exercise, and self-care matter more now. I always knew that, but incorporating it all seemed more challenging when I was younger. Now I am older, I am trying to make a more conscious effort as my health is at the forefront.

Although I am not big, when it comes to social media. I have joined some support groups because I know I am not alone on this journey. Women need to keep talking and talking so this subject is always out there and acknowledged. We deserve to have trained healthcare professionals who have the knowledge and can support women in their struggles, so we do not have to suffer in silence or feel alone. I am happy, and I now see that I am not alone.

I am still working on myself and have made some lifestyle changes. I am still managing one hot flash at a time, working on my sleep, trying to find balance, and taking care of me. I understand this is all part of the journey. A journey which need not appear all that bad if we have education and support along the way. I've accepted my middle age and I now understand that my main priority should not be how I look visually, as I'm not trying to impress anyone. I will not try to be younger than I am because I do not need to be.

Instead, I will continue to view each day as a gift, no matter what or how it arrives, hot flashes and all. I am feeling more optimistic as I continue to research and figure out what is working for me. My highly anticipated menopause clinic appointment in September will enable me to see what options may be available for me. Menopause doesn't have to seem like it is all doom and gloom. I just wish there was more education. The important thing is to keep the conversation alive, as women's health really does matter.